RACHEL BROWNE
DANCING TOWARD THE LIGHT

Rachel Browne
Dancing Toward the Light

CAROL ANDERSON

PREFACE BY
GRANT STRATE

Cover design by Terry Gallagher/Doowah Design Inc.
Front cover photo from *Haiku* (choreography by Rachel Browne, 1971)
Photo by J. Coleman Fletcher
Carol Anderson's photo by Donna Griffith

The poem "The Unquiet Bed" and the excerpt from "Zambia: The Land" are from Dorothy Livesay's *Self-Completing Tree* (© 1986, 1999) and are reprinted with the kind permission of Beach Holme Publishing, Vancouver.

Published with the financial assistance of the Manitoba Arts Council and The Canada Council for the Arts.

Printed and bound in Canada

Canadian Cataloguing in Publication Data

Anderson, Carol
    Rachel Browne: dancing toward the light

Includes bibliographical references and index.
ISBN 1-896239-53-6

    1. Browne, Rachel 2. Contemporary Dancers Inc.
3. Dancers—Canada—Biography I. Title.

GV1785.B76A53 1999   792.8'092   C99-901310-6

for Rachel and all her daughters

Happy the self-completing tree
that brews, in secret,
its own seasons...

O wild fig tree
you dance in fire and ashes
over world's mouth
dance

—Dorothy Livesay
from "Zambia: The Land"

CONTENTS

Preface 11

Foreword... 13

I/   *Dreams*
Strawberry Mansion 15

II/   *Blues & Highs*
New York City 24

III/   *Old Times Now*
The Royal Winnipeg Ballet 36

IV/   *The Woman I Am*
Motherhood and Teaching 47

V/   *Songs and Dances*
Contemporary Dancers—The Beginning 53

VI/   *Variations*
Contemporary Dancers—Early Years and the School 67

VII/   *Continuum*
The Middle Years—Dancing Through the 1970's 78

VIII/   *Shalom*
A Coup 89

IX/   *A Jest of God*
New Beginnings.. 102

X/   *In a Dark Time the Eye Begins to See*
Hard Times and Changes at WCD 110

XI/   *Mouvement*
Mentor, Creator 116

XII/   *Edgelit* 132

Dance Works by Rachel Browne: A Chronology 147

Sources.. 157

Interviews and Acknowledgments... 161

Thanks 163

Index 165

PREFACE

Until I read this book, I thought I knew Rachel Browne. In fact, I thought I knew her very well. So this work by Carol Anderson has pleasantly surprised me by showing me much more of Rachel than I had known; even more satisfying, it has put Rachel's life of service to dance...and humanity...in a larger context. Despite the many hardships and setbacks Rachel has endured in her own life, she has never given up or chosen the easier path, as many of us might have. It occurred to me, while reading this well-deserved tribute to an amazing woman, that the few people I have known who share these qualities with Rachel Browne have all been women—women who knew they must fight harder to accomplish their dreams in a man's world but who have managed nonetheless to make contributions beyond gender.

Carol Anderson shares this feminist appreciation of Browne and her work. She writes of Browne's creative passions with understanding and compassion. She details the many transitions Browne experienced for her work to reach its present level of maturity and clarity. Throughout her long career as dancer, director, choreographer and relentless advocate, Browne's urge to create dances was always a primary motivation. But it was only after she had paid her often heavy dues as student, ballet dancer, modern dancer, artistic director, manager, fund-raiser and teacher that she was able to devote herself unequivocally to creation that speaks of herself, to herself, to women and danced by women. Although she made dances even in her student days and continued to do so through her many years as founding director of Contemporary Dancers, many of them memorable, her work deepened when she became an independent artist able to satisfy her own creative needs without trying to balance the needs of a repertory company. While the circumstances of becoming an independent artist were often painful, they provided rewards.

The early chapters of this book describe Rachel's immigrant lineage, the hardships of growing up as an only child and her relationship with her mother, Eva, who shared with Rachel her passion for the outdoors and music and instilled socialist values into her very bones. Eva remained a defining presence for Rachel until her death at age 94. Rachel's fierce determination to be a classical ballet dancer in her earlier years led her to Winnipeg, where she followed her teacher/mentor Benjamin Harvarky and began her professional dancing career with the fledgling Winnipeg Ballet. And in putting down the roots for modern dance Rachel Browne showed herself to be made of the same stuff as the immigrant pioneers who settled western Canada.

We owe a great deal to Rachel Browne. She is a role model for all of us, old and young. *Dancing Toward the Light* aptly illustrates her devotional life journey. I hope we can look forward to many more years of that journey.

Grant Strate, C.M.

FOREWORD

Through her abiding devotion to her art, Rachel Browne has come to stand as a moral force in Canadian dance. Singular in her courage, unwavering in her discipline and at times through sheer bloody-mindedness, Rachel has been a trailblazer of dance in Canada. Moving through her sixties, she is unique in this country. She is immersed in her evolving choreographic career and continues to be passionately involved with teaching and guiding younger artists.

Rachel has fought her way to this time of her life through doubt, adversity, poverty and sharp opposition. She has always fought the "Dance Establishment", including the company she started in 1964, Winnipeg's Contemporary Dancers. After twenty years of effort Contemporary Dancers dismissed her as artistic director. A succeeding director attempted to ban her from entering the company's studios. Remarkably, through her determination to do the right thing, she now enjoys a cordial relationship with the company, actively contributing to its artistic life as founding artistic director.

Rachel has fought for recognition. She fights the passage of time with equal determination. Maintaining a strict program of physical training helps her sustain the creative work and teaching which are her life. It also affords her the unusual perspective of being a senior dance creator who is still practising her discipline. Rachel has enriched those who work with her through her resolute artistic engagement. Yet her present creative ferment can hardly be called a time of grace.

She just will not quit.

Through the 1950s and 1960s Rachel's complicated woman/mother/leader/dancer/teacher conundrum confounded her creative urges. She spent long years busy with the demands of her company. Yet, paradoxically, she felt artistically compromised by her struggle to balance the claims of the company she had started. Her ideals for the Contemporary Dancers often entailed putting her own creative needs last.

Ballet was Rachel's muse from early childhood. It was the foundation of her belief in dance. As a child and as a young woman she was a devout ballet dancer who practiced obsessively. Her training went deep into her body and psyche. Harmony, symmetry, musicality and a composed notion of beauty were expressed through the early dances she made.

Contemporary dance has been Rachel's partner on a long passage of discovery. In earlier creations she was constrained by her desire to fulfill the needs of dancers, of her company's repertory and of the boards of directors who caused her such grief through over-zealous involvement with the Contemporary Dancers. Through a steadfast commitment to creating dances, she has found a way to create in recent years which is not formulaic, but austere, deeply personal and emotionally resonant.

Rachel is interested in all manifestations of women's lives through her art. She speaks about areas which fascinate and provoke her, delving into the primal roots of emotional gesture. She looks into dark, quiet moments in the emotional topography of women's lives. She wrestles with the complex tangle of obsession, sweetness, naiveté and toughness which is her nature and the ground of her vision. Her bemused, honest, obstinate struggle toward an authentic voice is the soul of a mature artist.

Rachel has earned wisdom. Pain and commitment, change and loyalty, have marked her personal life and have changed her art. Hardship and striving seem to have cleared her way to the bright flame of her art and life. She has endured, developing the voice in which she expresses her vision.

She seems raku-fired. Colours of the earth, unpredictable, rich and deep, burnish her love of movement. She projects intense, dynamic density through her appetite to be moved and to speak, through her respect for dance artists of all ages.

Rachel's life and art have had several clear epochs. Through her whole life runs the delicate, indestructible golden thread of her determination to mature as a woman dance artist and to speak her truth. One thing is always true. Rachel Browne loves dance as her life.

STRAWBERRY MANSION

Rachel was born Ray Minkoff in Philadelphia on November 6, 1934. She grew up in a downscale part of Philadelphia euphemistically known as "Strawberry Mansion". Her parents were Russian immigrants. Rachel's mother Eva Greenberg left Russia in 1925. Rachel's father Israel Minkoff was a White Russian with revolutionary ideals. Though she had half-brothers and sisters by an earlier marriage of her father's, these siblings were much older and did not live with Rachel and her parents.

Rachel remembers her childhood as a time of indulgence. Adored as an only child, she was denied nothing, though her parents were by no means wealthy. Looking back, she feels that her childhood was very healthy. She feels that her upbringing gave her a foundation of confidence, a belief that it was in her power to have what she desired.

Rachel's mother worked as a seamstress in a garment factory. She was simultaneously independent and subservient to her husband. Rachel recalls Eva living her life "her own way", sitting in the park when she wanted to, not bound by expectations. Rachel traces her continuing need for finding solace in nature to childhood afternoons with her mother in the park. All her life Rachel has needed connection with nature, whether walking by the ocean shore in her New York City days, or today at her Willow Island retreat on Lake Winnipeg.

Because of her mother's low earnings and long hours, Rachel attended a day care centre, then called a "Day Nursery", with the assistance of a subsidy. She loved it, content to be with other children all day, never feeling sad to be separated from her parents. The children had a music and rhythm class during which they played various instruments. During these musical activities her teacher noticed Rachel's precocious rhythmic talent and suggested to her mother that she have music lessons.

Rachel was taken to music lessons at The Settlement Music School, part of Philadelphia's renowned Curtis Institute. These early lessons, given her parents' modest lifestyle, must have meant sacrifice for them. She recalls how "…every Saturday, we would take a long, long trolley ride down to south Philadelphia and I would have my lesson." As well, Eva took her daughter to the opera and to the symphony on Saturdays.

Rachel's musical study was in a sense a foundation of her dancing. The love of great music continues to be a source of her creativity. She continued her piano studies until she was a teenager. After she left The Settlement School a private teacher introduced her to music by Puccini and Verdi. Rachel recalls playing music from *La Bohème*. Her parents managed to scrape money together for these years of lessons and for the purchase of a second-hand piano, which was carefully tuned. "A conscientious kid", she practiced regularly until she was fifteen or sixteen. She recalls gossamer dreams of becoming a concert pianist.

Rachel was smitten by the desire to dance when she was a tiny girl. She remembers a dancer who came to her school. The girl was wearing socks over her pointe shoes and dancing on her toes. Mystified and enthralled, Rachel told her mother she wanted to study that kind of dancing. There was a dance school on the corner of their street, the Mimi School of Ballet, a private studio run by two sisters. It was not thriving, so Rachel is certain that her family must have paid for those lessons. Her mother found a way to give her little daughter this opportunity. Every week she took tap and ballet classes, as well as elocution lessons, and she participated in the annual concerts. From the time she was no more than six years old, Rachel has been dancing.

Rachel vividly remembers her mother sewing costumes for her, sitting up late in the lamplight. Eva stitched "a red satin outfit with gold stripes and long pants, a typical Oriental-looking jacket and a beautiful crown" for a "Chinese dance" in one of the school's annual concerts. Rachel recalls her mother being very creative with ribbons and costume jewellery, sewing them into her costume, which did double duty on Hallowe'en. Eva mother was to help and support her daughter in direct, self-sacrificing ways all the rest of her life.

Rachel adored her mother and felt very close to her. Eva was not well educated, having gone to school in Russia to the end of Grade 2 or 3. She came from a background of abject poverty. She told Rachel about how, having nothing to wear on her feet, she found a pair of old men's shoes and stuffed them with newspapers so she could walk to school in the winter. After the Russian Revolution, when education became more widely available, Eva trained as a nurse. While waiting to emigrate to the United States she was detained in London, England for three or four years during the late 1920's. She loved London and its museums.

During this time of transition she taught herself English by reading the English dictionary and books by Charles Dickens. Rachel recalls that her mother's English was virtually accent-free and that she had a wonderful ear for languages. When she arrived in Philadelphia, she enrolled in English classes and soon graduated from English high school. Rachel recalls finding fragments of her mother's writing dating from soon after her arrival in America, sensitive fragments that suggested a writer's soul.

Rachel remembers clearly how her mother helped her while she was a schoolgirl. When Rachel had to write a composition about the snow for homework one evening, her mother's suggestions for subject matter were poetic, images of snowflakes sparkling under streetlamps late at night.

Eva had an innate artistic sensibility. She was musical and had a beautiful singing voice. In fact she met Rachel's father while both were members of a Philadelphia choir. There was no opportunity for her to pursue her artistic inclinations once she was married and working. Conventions were very different then, even though Rachel's parents were hardly typical American parents. Her mother was a talented free spirit and her father respected her independence, yet both lived inside firm expectations of the roles which married people took on.

Rachel's father was much older than his wife. Though the father and daughter liked one another, they generally kept out of one another's way. But when Rachel questioned him, her father would talk quite freely about his own past. Despite the difficulties of their life in America, Rachel's parents were sustained by their political beliefs. Rachel recalls her father telling her that he had to leave Russia. His wealthy parents bribed the authorities so that he would not be thrown into jail for his revolutionary beliefs and agreed to send him to America. Israel Minkoff was an exile in the United States. His inability to return to his homeland was clearly a sorrow for the rest of his life.

"My mother used to make fun of him, that his pockets were always stuffed full of periodicals. He read newspapers and journals, and listened to short-wave radio…Whatever he read that came out of the Soviet Union, he believed implicitly that this was truth…My mother was very left wing too… They were on the side of the Revolution."

Rachel's mother was less fervent politically than her father. An avid reader even when Rachel was tiny, Eva was keenly interested in her books and novels. Israel read voraciously, taking his politics through journals. Rachel remembers him reading the Communist newspaper *The Daily Worker*. She remembers taking the bus with her mother to the library and coming out with armloads of books. Her parents loved good music. The radio in their household was always tuned to classical works.

Rachel reflects that her father's emotions emerged most freely in response to music. Eva told her how his eyes would fill with tears when he listened to Paul Robeson, the great singer, with his songs of long-suffering strength in the face of injustice. Systemic prejudice and injustice remained the core of black experience in post-Depression America. Rachel's father was profoundly moved by Robeson's songs of the oppressed. He might have heard his own Russian sympathies echoed in Robeson's brave thunder.

Rachel's ideology and politics are an integral part of her dance creation. Her beliefs have guided her philosophically in issues as fundamental as what kind of company she would form, and what works the company would perform. She was influenced profoundly by the social issues which wove through her carefree girlhood. Her early life, through all her dancing and music and reading, was marked by a thread of questioning. She remembers this as a constant theme of conversation in her home.

"In the war time, and as far back as I can remember…everything was questioned. I grew up being very wary of the U.S. government… I remember I would try to explain to my friends why communism was better, more humane than capitalism. In high school I used to go on peace marches and wherever there were protests."

Perhaps this early basis of questioning everything has fed Rachel's artistic evolution. A constant sense of revisiting issues, refining one's perception and expression, and an ability to consider things in radical form are essential to the creative process.

As a teenager Rachel attended the Girls' High School in Philadelphia. This was a very conservative school, with a classical slant on education, and the aim of preparing young women for university. The school had a peace club, of which Rachel was a member. They discussed the horrors of war. The teacher, a Miss Duncan, was a pacifist and, Rachel recalls, a vegetarian.

Rachel also went to the Sholem Aleichem Folk Schul, an alternative progressive Jewish School, to learn Yiddish. She recalls a good deal of discussion about politics, about the benefits of socialism, and about the evils of capitalism. There were cultural influences at the Schul as well. The students had chorus, where they learned singing. They also studied modern dance with a Philadelphia dance pioneer named Elfrieda Mahler. Mahler went to Cuba at the beginning of the revolution to live and support the revolution's work through her art by giving concerts, forming companies and teaching dance in remote areas. Many years later, while on holiday in Cuba, Rachel travelled to Havana to visit Elfrieda Mahler. She found her living in comparative ease, well provided for, still devoted to the ideals of Castro's Cuba. She was still actively animating dance activity in villages and cities throughout her adopted country.

While in Philadelphia Elfrieda Mahler gave solo concerts and enjoyed a certain notoriety as the city's "revolutionary" modern dancer. Rachel recalls her creating a work and inviting Rachel to contribute by improvising or making up a section. Rachel remembers not being able to think of anything creative to do, thinking that a beautiful, stylized arabesque line was the solution. Yet she was encouraged by Mahler all the same.

The Schul also gave annual variety programs, including dance, music and some drama. Once a well-known Jewish director came in to stage a play in Yiddish. On the strength of Rachel's innate ability to put herself into the character of an old woman, she was cast in a lead role as the mother. She remembers being coached and encouraged through the rehearsal process, and learning a great deal.

Rachel does not recall knowing anyone else like herself among their working-class neighbours. She remembers the Minkoffs as being rather isolated. Her mother had friends with whom she sat in the park, but the family did not have social gatherings at home. Occasionally they visited with her father's children, two half-brothers and a half-sister, who were married with children of their own.

Though Rachel was cherished by her family and given every opportunity to follow her artistic impulses, her parents' lives were hard, and were edged with tragedy. Her father worked as an insurance agent and occasionally sold real estate, but never seemed to make very much money. Strawberry Mansion began to change. The working-class Jewish neighbourhood started to fill with black families. As the area changed, racial enmity moved in. One night Rachel's father came home bleeding. He had been brutally attacked while collecting money for insurance policies in one of the very poor neighbourhoods. After this beating, he never truly recovered his health.

The image of Israel Minkoff that night, badly injured, begging forgiveness for his attackers, endured with Rachel's mother.

"My mother, right to the end of her life, remembered clearly how he came home and she got a big basin. She was sitting at the table and he was bleeding into the basin. She was going to call the doctor and my father was saying in Yiddish 'Forgive them, they don't know what they're doing' ...A socialist-communist right to the end."

⁒   ⁒   ⁒

The guiding light in Rachel's training was ballet. She describes herself as a "bunhead", and a very dedicated one at that. She worked with a physique that in her assessment was less than perfect for classical ballet. She knew she had a great sense of rhythm and a good sense of movement. But quite early, she knew she did not have the hyper-mobile flexibility which gives many ballerinas their gravity-defying extremity of range, their six o'clock penchés and the ability to extend their legs over their heads.

Rachel put her head down and applied herself to overcoming physical limitations. She is the first to use the word obsessive. To some degree this is part of any good dancer's makeup—tenacity is required, perfectionism is a positive value. In Rachel, boundless physical determination has been a driving force.

She remembers practising wherever she found an appropriate place. At home she used to hang onto the bottom of her parents' bed, the only available barre in their small apartment—until one night she watched, mortified, as the bed collapsed. Some nights she went back to the studio where she took her classes. She would get in through a window and practice late, going over and over her tendues and pliés, développés and frappés, re-doing the adagios and enchaînements from classes earlier in the day, intent on perfecting the movement detail of the ballet vocabulary. She was determined to get it right into the fibre of her young muscles. She wanted to be perfect.

Rachel had switched from her local school to the Littlefield Ballet School, started by Catherine Littlefield, one of Philadelphia's early ballerinas. While she was a student at this school she began performing. She appeared in classical studies and in some character work. Rachel had her first taste of great ballet here, which whetted her appetite for more.

As a young teenager, she had thought she would find a profession which would allow her to follow the love of nature she had absorbed from her mother. She might become a teacher, she thought, so she could take the summers off, swim and go out into the country. By the time she was sixteen or seventeen, though, Rachel was determined to dance. She remembers reading Agnes de Mille's *Dance to the Piper* at this time. In this inspiring, if cautionary tale of her own early dance life, de Mille describes how she practiced devotedly, obsessively, to the point of injury.

Rachel recalls telling the director of the local dance school that she wanted to be a dancer. The teacher was extremely dubious. She gave Rachel some movement phrases to do, to see how she coped, and tried to dissuade her without actually telling her not to go, telling her how very difficult it was to dance in New York.

Despite the lack of encouragement, Rachel decided to be a dancer. She was bolstered by the confidence in herself which her upbringing had built. She was driven by her love of dance. And she was young. She believed in her power to create her own life.

Rachel found out through Catherine Littlefield's school that Antony

Tudor was going to give a series of Sunday workshops in Philadelphia. Tudor's dance life began in England, but he soon moved on to a wide-ranging choreographic career. By the mid-1940's, the British choreographer was revered, and feared, in the international ballet world.

Tudor was the originator of a new genre of dance. His "psychological ballets" brought the world such moody, brilliant works as *Lilac Garden*, *Dark Elegies* and *Pillar of Fire*. His work stemmed from the well-bred idiom of British ballet. Yet it was the way his dances tapped the emotional qualities of music through phrasing and dynamics which strongly influenced ballet choreography at mid-century. Tudor's ballets reached outward, placing their characters in context of their communities. His works threw light into the last shadows of emotional constraint which had dulled ballet expression since Edwardian times. His probing acuity did not stop with his dance works. He had a fearsome reputation for occasional cruelty, particularly in comments to young women dancers.

Having Antony Tudor work in Philadelphia was an important event in the city's lively cultural scene. He was to mount a production of *Les Sylphides*. It was to take place at the Academy of Music and be performed with the Philadelphia Orchestra under the direction of Eugene Ormandy. Rachel leapt at the chance to work with Tudor.

"This was an opportunity to work with a great master, so I went to his classes, which I thought were strange and quirky…It was true that he had a very, very sharp side. He could be quite cruel in his criticisms. I noticed that he paid lots of attention to some of the people that had ideal dancer bodies, not that much attention to me, though he did help me. He did put me in the production…I remember the kind of direction we got. It was quite a revelation, very sophisticated direction. It wasn't just a bunch of steps but a certain ambience and mood that we had to capture, very romantic, wispy…"

Rachel gathered her courage and spoke to Tudor. Although he had not been unkind to her, he had not encouraged her. She did not dare to ask him whether he felt that she had the potential to become a dancer, as she did not want to hear a negative answer. Instead, she asked his advice about where to study in New York. She had decided to go. "I just knew that I wanted to go," she recalls, "and that's exactly what I did."

Rachel's intensity has a way of commanding respect and attention.

She recalls Tudor answering her questions about New York City with consideration. Perhaps, she reflects, he could see where her talents lay, for he guided her toward teachers in New York who were evolving a contemporary use of ballet in the mid-1950s. He recommended a number of teachers to her including Edward Caton, Robert Joffrey and Benjamin Harkarvy, who was to become Rachel's mentor and main teacher.

Although this was a brief encounter, Rachel long remembered Tudor's direction for *Les Sylphides*. His unique musicality was the key to the emotional life of his ballets. His aim of creating a certain atmosphere through musicality and movement detail was later to find a reflection in the attentiveness of her own direction.

Rachel's musical understanding, cultivated since early childhood, has been a deep source in her dances. It is intriguing to wonder at the way in which this meeting with Tudor, which took place at an impressionable point in Rachel's dance life, seeded her later experience. Somewhere in her mind an ideal of dance as an expressive, eloquently musical world began to germinate and move toward the light.

NEW YORK CITY

The day after she graduated from high school, Rachel moved to New York City. She was seventeen and a half. When Rachel told her parents that she had decided to be a dancer and wanted to move to New York, they thought she was mad. But they did not try to obstruct her. In their eyes, she was her own boss. Before she left home, her father had placed ads in the *New York Times* advertising her services as a part-time typist, so she arrived in New York with a job. "I don't think it lasted very long," reflects Rachel, "because I wasn't a very good typist…"

She was uninterested in the typing and clerical work she did. She had taught herself typing in her last year of high school. She was intelligent and could spell and compose letters with ease. However, her jobs, one of the first in a firm which sold a blemish cover cream, others now forgotten, were nothing more than a means of surviving.

Rachel launched into an exhilarating whirl of activity, patching together a schedule of work and two ballet classes a day. She had very little money and constantly scrambled to pay for her classes, pay her rent, and eat. One of her typing jobs brought her in touch with a cult headed by a charismatic figure who styled himself "Father Divine". Members of the group took new names such as "Truelove", and lived communally, segregated by sex.

Rachel's interest in this organization was strictly based on the huge weekend dinners they gave to attract new members. These were quite convenient to her apartment. She roomed with a girlfriend, Gloria Spivak, from Philadelphia, who had danced with Elfrieda Mahler and studied with Alwin Nikolais in New York. The girls rented a room in the home of a Yiddish teacher they knew who had left their Philadelphia Schul and was living in Harlem, at 116th Street and Lexington Avenue.

"I was living on peanut butter sandwiches, which made me nice and hefty but I wasn't being properly nourished. The food at the weekend recruiting meetings was phenomenal, a major feast, and I was so hungry that I just stuffed myself..." She recalls the cult members being quite put out when they discovered the underlying reason for her attendance.

Her parents tried to persuade her to move out of Harlem to a less dangerous part of town. Rachel thought she was fine where she was and applied herself to doing the rounds of the New York studios, seeking out teachers and potential dance jobs. Her schedule was to dance in her classes during the day and work at night. While she was in New York she studied with many teachers, among them Benjamin Harkarvy, Edward Caton, Robert Joffrey, and teachers at the American Ballet Theatre. She worked hard in her two classes a day, wanting to get the most from every minute of study. She practiced in between classes too, a self-described fanatic.

Rachel was convinced that she could become a star.

Benjamin Harkarvy was teaching classes at Carnegie Hall, a honeycomb of studios and studio apartments. It was rumoured that Marlon Brando kept an apartment there. Rachel was thrust into the electricity of living in New York, revelling in the charge which could be felt from the concentrated energies of so many ambitious, talented, hungry, aspiring artists.

Rachel describes being starved and exhausted all the time, running from job to class to school, pointe shoes hanging out of her bag, eating lunch from a brown paper bag while she rode the subway. She describes this period in New York as chaste and cloistered. The whole focus of her life was her dance classes. She would go to her first class of the day. After the class she practiced until her energy was completely spent, going over and over the exercises.

Then she would head for the Horn & Hardart Automat. This

automated cafeteria was a New York City phenomenon. Large banks of glass-fronted cabinets offered different items, such as sandwiches, jello or fruit. The diner inserted coins, a couple of quarters or dimes, in the window in front of her choice, opened the front and took out the selection. Rachel remembers always needing to eat and always needing to scrimp. She would insert money for a hard-boiled egg, or go for rye bread, because you could get more than two slices. She and a friend often made themselves lemon drinks with free glasses of water, ice and lemon slices. After refuelling, she travelled to whatever temporary work she was doing. Then she returned to 57th Street and 7th Avenue for her second class at Carnegie Hall. Sometimes these were night classes. Rachel remembers the custodial staff making their rounds and having to kick her out. She might otherwise have stayed in the hallway outside the studio practising all night.

Rachel took in ballet performances whenever she could manage to pay for a ticket. She went to see the New York City Ballet and the American Ballet Theatre at City Center on 55th Street. Lincoln Center, "the new place", was not yet open. In time-honoured, poverty-stricken dancer fashion, Rachel would buy a cheap seat, high up at the top of the theatre; at intervals, she would gradually move closer to the stage.

All of the performances she saw were food to her ardour for the ballet. Rachel was starry-eyed. Yet she has always been a discerning viewer of dance, and watching ballet in New York steeped her in ideas about beauty and craft. The American Ballet Theatre was performing many of Tudor's ballets including *Jardin aux Lilas*, *Dark Elegies* and *Dim Lustre*, perhaps also Agnes de Mille's *Fall River Legend*. Works by George Balanchine, *Apollo* and *Ballet Imperial* and *Symphony in C*, as well as classics such as *Giselle* and *Les Sylphides,* were on their programs. The New York City Ballet's performances in the mid-1950's included repertory by Balanchine, such as *The Four Temperaments*, *Episodes*, *Serenade*, *Concerto Barocco* and *Allegro Brillante,* and Jerome Robbins' *Fancy Free*. Rachel had the opportunity to see great dance stars of the time, among them Melissa Hayden, Allegra Kent, Violette Verdy, Jacques d'Amboise, perhaps Erik Bruhn, Kay Mazzo, Patricia McBride, maybe even Alicia Alonso.

"A total ballet freak" during this time in New York, Rachel avoided performances of modern dance, which she considered ugly. Had she been drawn to it then, she would have seen Martha Graham, still in her heyday, watched the beginnings of Paul Taylor's and Merce Cunningham's careers as choreographers, and perhaps seen the great humanist works of José Limón danced by his company.

Despite her fervent devotion to ballet, Rachel was not without early contact with modern dance and dancers. She was an earnest young woman, eager to put her political convictions to work. Soon after her arrival in New York she became part of a group of like-minded young dancers, including her friend Harriet Gendel, who styled themselves The New Century Dancers. Rachel considered herself politically enlightened, taking a stand against greed and capitalism. She and the other members of the dance group, who were both ballet and modern dancers, agreed that membership would be restricted to those who believed in socialism or communism. She remembers a discussion with a renowned Marxist theorist who visited the group to discuss culture and Marxism with the young dancers. He was rather amused by their zeal and suggested that they could perhaps loosen their membership criteria a little.

The group gave some performances in the Lower East Side, in the theatre of the Jewish Educational Alliance, a lively community centre. One of the performers, who appeared with The New Century Dancers and made a lasting impression on Rachel, was a man named Irving Burton. Although Burton was a fine dancer, trained in the Graham style, he was not invited to appear with the Martha Graham company, Rachel recounts, because his baldness did not fit that company's aesthetic. The New Century Dancers invited him to perform with them. Rachel recalls wryly that he was the only man in The New Century Dancers and was appointed director. Burton created some politically pointed works. Rachel describes one about judges and victims. The dancers wore masks, and the work took a very strong political point of view, condemning the evils of the McCarthy era. The connection with Burton was to endure, for Rachel invited his niece Rosalind Newman, "a wonderful choreographer", to create a work for Contemporary Dancers many years later. Although Rachel eschewed modern dance, there was a connection from her first days in New York.

A sense of fearlessness still emanates from Rachel's first time in New York. She took the opportunity to try anything that attracted her. Her earliest choreographic experience was gained with The New Century Dancers. In one of these early performances she choreographed a piece to Mozart country dances. Benjamin Harkarvy attended the performance. Rachel remembers his pleased, surprised response to her work. He remarked on its musicality and on the loveliness of the choreography. The work was not political in any way, but Rachel recalls not seeing any real contradiction between her politics and her dancing. It was part of her conviction that ballet dancers could be progressive thinkers, hold political ideals and dance at the same time.

Although busy with work and dance study, Rachel felt committed to extending her education in other ways. She was still very interested in Jewish studies and politics. Her reading of Marx and Engels was part of her world view. Looking back, she believes that it was in fact part of her education as an artist. "I realize, in retrospect," she says, "that to become a professional dancer one has to be highly, highly intelligent—to be able to retain all the things that one has to learn in order to perform and then to have the sensitivity and emotional wherewithal to be expressive as well."

Rachel had to relinquish the idea of delving into Jewish studies because she simply did not have the time to learn Yiddish or study the literature in depth. Instead she enrolled in a class at the School for Social Research, a Manhattan night school with a Marxist orientation. She met Don Browne, her first husband, there. He remembers her rushing in, always late from her job or her ballet class, trailing ribbons and dance clothes.

After the first or second class Don invited Rachel to join him for a meal. On this first date Rachel and Don went to the Automat, which was convenient and inexpensive. Though he was astonished by how much she ate, it was Don's treat. Rachel recalls him spending a lot of money on feeding her, as she was always hungry. She describes this as a time when she started to develop strange eating patterns. She was always wanting to lose weight, but needed energy and had no money. She recalls, for instance, that she would eat huge amounts of starch, bread, cereal, potatoes, first thing in the morning but then not again all day, thinking that the calories would be burned up during the day. Or she would eat a small box of raisins from a corner deli, knowing that they were an energy food, and had iron in them.

Rachel recalls Harkarvy and his partner suggesting that she lose a little weight by eating more healthily. She remembers a stretch of time when she frequently ate liver. Years later, when she discovered how high in cholesterol it is, she was aghast. While she was living with Don, she recalls, she would go home at night, and cook liver and vegetables. But every two days or so, when she had the money, she would buy herself a cheese Danish at Ratner's, a famous dairy restaurant on Delancey Street. This was a favourite treat. Gradually, her weight dropped from about 125 pounds to about 112 pounds. At the time, she says, this was considered quite thin.

At the age of eighteen and a half, Rachel decided to marry Don Browne. He was about eleven years older than she. Rachel remembers looking up to him as a mature, experienced companion. Their shared political beliefs were a bond. Rachel admired him for his generosity toward her and others. He was very supportive of her. He believed in Rachel's talent and used to tell his friends that she was one of the most exceptional dancers in New York.

Rachel and Don got married in the New York City registry office. Afterward, they caught a bus to Philadelphia, where Eva threw a party for her daughter and her new husband. Their guests were Rachel's friend Harriet Gendel and her husband, some of Rachel's family members and other New York friends. Rachel remembers that it was hot in Philadelphia, boiling hot as they partied in her parents' small downstairs apartment. Afterward, she and Don took a short honeymoon trip to the mountains before returning to New York.

The Brownes lived in a cheap apartment at 99 Suffolk Street, near the corner of Delancey. Rachel remembers the vitality of the historic Lower East Side, which had been home to the first Jewish immigrants in New York City. By the time she lived there the streets were brimming with spicy Puerto Rican culture. Many years later she went back to her old neighbourhood to look for the building, but found that it had been demolished.

The Browne's Suffolk Street apartment was infested with roaches. It was a cold water flat with the toilet in the hallway outside. A "railroad" flat, all its rooms were lined up along one interior hall. The bathtub was attached to the kitchen sink. "During the day, we covered it with a board," recalls Rachel. "You could take a bath if you took off the board but during the day you used it as a place to put various things, books or dishes."

Twice, while she and Don lived on Suffolk Street, they woke to smoke and flame and sirens in the middle of the night. Twice, they found themselves huddled in the street while firemen doused their burning apartment building. As a result, Rachel is phobic about fire. She is wary of electricity, and checks the stove with care. During her touring days with Contemporary Dancers, she always selected a room close to the fire escape, and checked for fire exits before settling in. Once she found herself trapped outside a locked fire door on a second-floor hotel roof late at night and had to jump down. "Just a few scratches," she maintains. Even now, she confesses, she rehearses her escape route from hotel rooms in case of fire.

The Brownes moved to the Bronx to escape the firetrap. Rachel describes how she soon began to feel itchy and agitated, and wonder if she was ill. She woke up one night in their new apartment, feeling bitten. Rising to turn on the light, Rachel and Don discovered the mattress running red with bedbugs gorged on Rachel's blood. They had not bitten Don. Horrified, the Brownes fled to the house of Rachel's friend Harriet Gendel, riding the subway in the middle of the night to Brooklyn. It was a dangerous and frightening ride, remembers Rachel, but there was no alternative—she could not bear to stay in their infested apartment.

During the first years of their marriage, Rachel and Don joined a Communist Party club. Don, she recalls, decided to join the Longshoremen's Union. He had trained as a lawyer. His aim was to put his university education and his socialist sympathies to work, to educate and enlighten workers in the Longshoremen's Union while he loaded grain. Rachel was thrilled when the Brownes qualified to move to a subsidized building. It was clean, complete with beautiful floors that looked like hardwood, real rooms and hot and cold running water. The housing project was in an area of the Brooklyn docks called Red Hook.

Rachel recalls her parents coming to see her in New York, her mother arriving laden with dishes of chicken to feed her famished daughter. Her father was frail and the journey was difficult for him. Soon she and her mother took an occasional trip by subway to Brighton Beach to walk by the shore. If Rachel was visiting Philadelphia, she and her mother would travel by bus to Atlantic City. Rachel recalls that it always rained on these excursions.

On Sundays, Rachel and Don would sometimes ride the subway for an hour to Brooklyn. There they visited Harriet Gendel and enjoyed a short respite from the city. Another friend lived in New Jersey. Rachel sometimes travelled to see her, to sit and look at trees and greenery and walk outside. Rachel dreaded going back to the city, especially when the heat of summer shimmered over the ocean. Returning to New York felt like going back to a prison. She felt caged and oppressed by city grime and concrete. She missed green, growing things. Yet she always returned to New York, drawn by the dance.

Since early days, Rachel has been a working dancer. Driven by her urgency to perform, and by her need for money, she attended an arduous round of auditions for Broadway shows, the New York City Ballet, and American Ballet Theatre. She recalls nearly getting work with the American Ballet Theatre after performing in a choreographic workshop there. Finally, she acquired her Equity card by landing a job in a summer stock production of *Oklahoma!*, in which she danced reconstructed choreography by Agnes de Mille. Acquiring the card enabled Rachel to bypass the discouraging anonymity of "cattle calls", attended by hundreds of hopefuls, for the relative luxury of auditioning with only forty or fifty dancers at an Equity call.

Oklahoma! was significant for Rachel in another way too. When she went to collect her Equity card, she discovered that there was another "Ray Browne" already registered. So she became Rachel Browne.

During her New York years Rachel danced with the New York Dance Drama Company under the direction of Emily Frankel and Mark Ryder. She performed with them from 1954-56. Harkarvy had pointed her out when they came to watch his classes, looking for dancers. Their company performed both ballet and modern work. Frankel and Mark Ryder created in the modern idiom, as did guest choreographer Sophie Maslow, who had been an original member of the Martha Graham Dance Company. They also performed choreography by Zachary Solov, director of the Metropolitan Opera Ballet, and work by Todd Bolender, who had danced with the New York City Ballet and at that time was a well-known ballet choreographer. The Ryder-Frankel company toured extensively throughout the United States, undertaking demanding tours of two and three months' duration. They did many one-night stands. Rachel was ecstatic with this long-coveted opportunity to really get into performing.

"I remember relishing the touring, thinking every performance was heaven. My whole life was geared toward wanting to perform. We rehearsed in some kind of an upstairs loft. I remember being afraid that the place would burn down or some terrible disaster would occur, so that the opportunity to perform would be taken away..."

Even as she began touring and tasting the thrill of life on stage, Rachel's studies in New York continued to excite her. Many outstanding dancers attended classes with Harkarvy, the teacher to whom she now looked as a mentor. She recalls seeing Melissa Hayden and Allegra Kent in class, as well as Glen Tetley, John Butler, and luminaries from Martha Graham's company, including Mary Hinkson and Ethel Winter.

As her mentor, Rachel chose a high achiever. Benjamin Harkarvy has had a very distinguished dance career. He has been a guest teacher at the Royal Danish Ballet, the Joffrey Ballet, in Israel at Bat d'Or and Batsheva, for the Ballet Rambert and for the Frankfurt Ballet. He has directed numerous companies, including the Royal Winnipeg Ballet, the Pennsylvania Ballet and the Harkness Ballet, and has choreographed for many European and American companies. His career has brought a modern point of view to ballet. In 1959 he was the founder of the Netherlands Dance Theatre and directed that company for the next ten years. The Netherlands Dance Theatre was the first company to call on the very highest standards in both modern and ballet training. Its phenomenal success was based on the superb dancers who gravitated to the company's challenges and on the fact that every work in the repertory was by a living choreographer. Harkarvy is the current director of dance at New York's Juilliard School, where he has for many years been a teacher and choreographer.

Harkarvy inspired Rachel. She describes his approach to ballet training—the "direct striving for unmannered simplicity"—as suited to her own physicality and taste. She had confidence in his eye for "organic, uncluttered placement". She felt her technique strengthen and deepen with his teaching. She also often took class with Robert Joffrey. She recalls that both were truly breaking ground with their teaching. They replaced the autocratic style of some of the Russian teachers in New York with an approach which attempted to explain and enlighten while training intelligent, healthy dancers. Rachel remembers that they verbalized reasons for particular movements and explained principles of placement which elsewhere were too often reduced to commands to, "Pull up. Get your leg up."

As well, Rachel attributes a good deal of her musical taste to what she heard in Harkarvy's classes.

"Harkarvy hired Juilliard students and accomplished pianists, and they played Bach. He would create combinations to this music that were so musical that they just came alive, they sang. He had exceptional taste and knowledge of music. I remember him talking about Edith Piaf and I remember the kind of music that he used. Mostly Bach, sometimes Schubert lieder, and I'm sure Mozart, but Bach was a great favourite. It influenced me greatly in my own musical tastes and in the kind of music I chose for classes. It almost made me into a musical snob. I would demand of pianists that I worked with that they play exceptional music, something that would develop the musical taste of the dancers."

Rachel describes listening to Harkarvy's conversations with the stars who studded his classes. After classes she lingered, doing tendues and eavesdropping a little, overhearing his critiques and opinions of various choreographies and performances. Occasionally he coached Melissa Hayden or Allegra Kent in their variations while Rachel hung about practising. She was a sponge, soaking it up. Her experiences with Harkarvy, "truly an innovative teacher", left indelible artistic impressions. Once in a great while Rachel summoned her courage and invited him to join her for a meal. Spellbound, she listened to the flow of his ideas and opinions. Only in recent years, she says, has she dared to disagree with him.

Although he was only twenty-six years old when he took on the directorship of the Royal Winnipeg Ballet, Harkarvy had exacting standards in both ballet and modern dance and a commitment to original creation. He seemed to see keenly into Rachel's qualities as a dancer and into her aspirations for her dance career.

At his invitation, Rachel accompanied Harkarvy when he went to Winnipeg to direct the Royal Winnipeg Ballet in 1957. Deciding whether or not to leave New York was very troublesome for Rachel. She had to grapple with her ideals and aims in a realistic way. She felt that New York City was the hub of the dance world and the centre of ballet, and was where she rightfully should be. She had gone to New York to study with the finest teachers. As she got deeper into serious study she began to have real doubts about her own physical limitations, yet she was determined to succeed. She was offered a six-month contract in Winnipeg. Finally she decided that she would go, but only for this short stretch of time. Then she would rush back to New York with new performance experience to add to her curriculum vitae, and renewed determination to "make it".

Rachel's sustaining goal had been to dance in a ballet company in New York. Her brushes with modern dance had been so far no more to her than a way of gaining performance experience. She had worked like a fiend to overcome a physical makeup which was not ideal for classical ballet. She had encouraged herself with stories of great dancers who overcame limitations. Alexandra Danilova is one artist she mentions. Harkarvy made an example to Rachel of how Danilova, even though she did not have high extensions, made exquisite use of her turnout and beautiful feet. Rachel explains:

"I definitely did not have the kind of limber body that was needed for a real classical dancer. I did have good feet. I was very, very musical and highly intelligent and able to pick up movement very quickly.

Harkarvy, who has exceptional standards in terms of the ballet aesthetic, understood my talent. He didn't just see me as a body, he saw how I could move, saw my expressiveness. That's why he asked me to join the Winnipeg Ballet. So I did, in a sense, achieve part of my goal."

Though she left the city with trepidation, promising herself a speedy return, Rachel never lived in New York again. Winnipeg and dance claimed her for new roles.

THE ROYAL WINNIPEG BALLET

Winnipeg in the 1950s was a centre of Prairie Canada, but to a Manhattan girl it must have looked flat and almost unbelievably empty. Rachel recalls landing at the old airport and looking at the endless horizon and the scattered airplane hangars. It was September 8, 1957, the end of a long, hot summer. She took in the scrubby trees and the depth of blue sky and the huge, pervasive silence. Kathleen Richardson, long-time board member and supporter of the Royal Winnipeg Ballet, met Rachel and dancer Richard Rutherford. She drove them down Main Street into Winnipeg.

"I looked at this desolate street and I thought, 'Where have I come to?'" Even more than forty years later, there is a note of despair in Rachel's voice as she remembers her dismay at her first sight of her new home, so very different from delicatessens and the subway, yellow taxis and the crowded sky of New York. The two dancers stayed at a small hotel on Portage Avenue, nursing their culture shock and listening to the boisterous sounds from the tavern downstairs.

Rutherford, originally from the southern United States, soon became a featured performer with the Royal Winnipeg Ballet. He created some thirty new roles in thirteen years, dancing with the company for the duration of his ballet career. Although Rachel and Rutherford did not know one another in New York, they soon became acquainted in Winnipeg as the life of the company, rehearsals, touring and performing, began to create common ground for them.

Rutherford fondly describes Rachel's quirkiness. Immediately, her preoccupation with practice highlighted her in the studio. When the company was on tour she continued to practice any time she could, backstage, in her hotel, in the wings. He describes her struggles to subdue her wiry hair into the requisite ballet bun. He remembers how resolutely Rachel wore the scratchy contact lenses of the time. She was the very image of the dutiful stage artist, seemingly prepared to endure any amount of discomfort for her art. Photographs of her with the ballet show her looking serene and long-necked, demure. She seems suffused with a kind of wilful beauty that speaks of her utter devotion to the image of the dancer.

Harkarvy became artistic director of the Royal Winnipeg Ballet during the company's long recovery from the destruction of its studios. The company lost all its costumes, sets, musical scores and archival materials, most of Gweneth Lloyd's choreographic notes among them, in June, 1954, when a devastating fire swept through downtown Winnipeg. Radical measures were taken to make the company's survival possible. Operations were suspended for many months and a fundraising campaign was started. The company did not perform again until November, 1955.

In 1956 the company hired Ruthanna Boris, a New York dancer and choreographer, who stayed on until 1957 to choreograph for the company. She expressed her aim to raise the level of the dancers' training, while she and her husband Frank Hobi were principal dancers with the company. Her professionalism was demanding and thorough, but Boris' sojourn at the Royal Winnipeg Ballet was divisive. By the early summer of 1957, Nenad Lhotka, long the ballet master, left and only two dancers remained with the company.

Benjamin Harkarvy was hired in August, 1957. Interestingly, 1957 was the year in which the Royal Winnipeg Ballet received its first Canada Council assistance. The grant was $20,000, and was one of the Council's first-ever grants to dance. The National Ballet of Canada also received a grant at this time, of $50,000. Entering what looked to be a new and golden era for the company, Harkarvy arrived in Winnipeg with six dancers, including Rachel and Richard Rutherford, and a music director, Richard Wernick.

The company's board of directors had by that time evolved and become used to an unusual rapport with the artistic side of the Royal Winnipeg Ballet. The close board-company alliance caused problems for Harkarvy almost immediately. He arrived with a two-year plan for the company, but it was never fully implemented. While he was with the company Harkarvy created or remounted four ballets.

One of the first works he rehearsed with the Royal Winnipeg Ballet was *La Primavera*. Rachel had danced in this work, set to the "Spring" section of Vivaldi's *The Four Seasons*, when Harkarvy showed his work at the Jacob's Pillow Dance Festival in the summer of 1957. The dance was well-received critically in Winnipeg, and optimistically hailed as reminiscent of the freshness of the company's earlier incarnations. Harkarvy created *The Twisted Heart* for the Royal Winnipeg Ballet in 1957, also for the November performances. Set to music composed by Richard Wernick, this was an adaptation of the *Pagliacci* story. *Four Times Six* was a light ballet set to music by Walter Mourant, which Harkarvy had created for a New York concert company. Harkarvy's *Fête Brillante*, set to music by Mozart, was designed as a showpiece for the company. *Fête Brillante* was choreographed early in 1958.

Rachel recalls feeling at first that she was very far away from New York. Once she became engrossed with the company, her longing for the city passed quickly. In fact she came to feel quite pleased that she was able to do classical work without the difficulty and hassle of living in New York. She was able to focus on her work in a concentrated way—the pace was very different than her Manhattan rush from class to audition to rehearsal. Dancing in a ballet company was all she wanted to do. In the Winnipeg company it was all she did, all she dreamed about, all she thought about.

Harkarvy's plan was to rebuild the company slowly. He wanted to create repertory in the first year, to maintain *Roundelay*, one of Ruthanna Boris' works, and to schedule a minimum of performances. His plan was to boost the performance and touring profile of the company in the second year, while continuing to refine the dancers' skills and build the company's reputation. The timing of Harkarvy's plan did not meet with full support from the Royal Winnipeg Ballet's board. Harkarvy wanted to nurture talent from within the company, while the board was keen to bring in guest artists. When ongoing tensions with the board made his directorship untenable, Harkarvy resigned abruptly in February of 1958, leaving before a series of performances which were to end the season in March. Arnold Spohr stepped in at that time. His directorship of the Royal Winnipeg Ballet was to continue for thirty years.

Rachel recalls Benjamin Harkarvy as an extraordinary director, subtle, skilled and very demanding. She had great confidence in his expertise, which made working with him a pleasure. During his time with the Royal Winnipeg Ballet it was his aim to build a repertory which the dancers truly understood; Rachel recalls his care and the close attention of his direction in rehearsals.

It must have been difficult for Rachel to watch Harkarvy leave Winnipeg, as he had been such an important influence on her dance career up to that point. She has always maintained a cordial rapport with him, visiting while she is in New York, and watching him teach. She continues to feel drawn to his refined and intellectual approach to dance, which affected her so deeply in her student days.

Rachel was a member of the Royal Winnipeg Ballet from 1957 to 1961. During her seasons with the company she danced in various works of the classic repertory, and as a soloist in *Bluebird Variations*. She danced the part of the cat in *Sleeping Beauty*. She also danced in works by Ruthanna Boris and Gweneth Lloyd. Rachel particularly mentions a role in Lloyd's work *Romance*, which she danced in her second year with the company. Set to Glazunov's *The Seasons*, she recalls it as a romantic, musical, somewhat old-fashioned ballet in which the girls wore long white tutus. She also danced in ballets by Brian Macdonald, as well as in Harkarvy's works during his time as director.

While Rachel was in the company, Arnold Spohr began to hit his stride as a director. He had a gift for recognizing talented young choreographers and invited them to work with the Royal Winnipeg Ballet. One of the first of these discoveries was Brian Macdonald. He was to become an important choreographer for the company, creating many landmark works including *Les Whoops-de-Doo* (1959), *Rose Latulippe* (1966), *Five Over Thirteen* (1969), and *The Shining People of Leonard Cohen* (1970).

Macdonald's first work for the Royal Winnipeg Ballet, *The Darkling*, was created in 1958. It was a great crowd-pleaser and became a repertory mainstay. It was set to Benjamin Britten's *Variations on a Theme of Frank Bridge*. Dramatic and compelling, the ballet looked at how inner compulsions and secrets can affect the happiness which people find with one another. Rachel was cast in *The Darkling*'s chorus, while her friend Marilyn Young, who was a prima ballerina with the company for eighteen years, was first-cast principal in the work.

Rachel inherited a role in *The Darkling* which had been originated by Olivia Wyatt, Brian Macdonald's wife. Rachel danced a duet, "The White Duet", with James Clouser. It was a soloist's role and she cherished it. She acutely recalls her understanding of the technique and the dramatic sensibility of the ballet. She found that she had a discerning instinct for what was needed dramatically. Her memory of *The Darkling* is as a highly inventive piece of choreography which was very challenging musically. Even then, though she burned to dance, she had a sense of the craft of choreography, and could to some extent stand outside work, considering its quality.

Working with the Winnipeg company was undeniably gruelling. Rachel had been disappointed by the small number of performances the company gave during her first year—only ten. She need not have worried. Determined to rebuild the company and make it financially viable and highly visible, Arnold Spohr charged into his new responsibilities and took the company on tour with the "Spohr mix"— programs which seemed to feature something to delight everyone. The company made a remarkable recovery. In 1959 it gave forty-two performances. In 1960 it made a tour of Western Canada and completed a 10,000-mile tour of Eastern Canada. In 1961 the company toured the northern and mid-west United States and Western Canada. During its 1960-61 season total attendance was 63,732.

The company made these mammoth North American tours by bus. There were no rules governing the dancers' travel and rest hours— they were not union members. Rachel recalls often climbing on the bus after a performance, driving many hours, resting briefly, performing, and travelling again; a loop of one-night stands that left many of the dancers injured and exhausted.

But Rachel, for the most part, was in her element. She describes sitting on the bus, singing to herself, looking at the scenery. "I was so delighted, thrilled out of my mind. I was travelling and looking at the world and dancing every night. Putting on my pointe shoes." She recalls Richard Rutherford making fun of her relentless cheerfulness.

The company travelled with two pianists who accompanied classes and performances. Spohr stood in the orchestra pit of the theatre when the company was performing, conducting the pianists and watching the dancers onstage at the same time. Rachel recalls Nancy Noonan, a fine, capable, high-strung pianist at times becoming so unnerved by Spohr's erratic conducting tempi that she lost her ability to speak.

Many of the theatres the Royal Winnipeg Ballet visited were small, underheated or overheated. Rachel remembers dancing on a stage in Medicine Hat. Where the wood ended, the rest of the stage was surfaced with a material which gave way when stepped on with a pointe shoe, so the women dancers sank in while on pointe or screwed themselves into the floor while turning. There were no crossovers, so the dancers had to run around outside the building and, of course, it was winter.

On its Medicine Hat program the company was performing *Ballet Premier*, a work made by Spohr, set to music by Mozart. At one point in the dance Rachel's partner put out his hands for her to join him in a long line of couples. Thoroughly disoriented by having run outside to make a crossover in the cold, Rachel was standing on the wrong side of the stage at the critical moment and did not make her entrance. Rachel thought this was hilarious, but the choreographer was not amused. She recalls that Spohr was absolutely furious and refused to speak to her for several days, though they travelled at close quarters on the bus.

Rachel recalls the choreography of *Ballet Premier* mirroring the structure of the Mozart score. When the work was remounted some years ago by the Royal Winnipeg Ballet, she remembered it intact from having performed it so many times.

Rachel thought that Spohr was a fine director, though in those early days she also found him idiosyncratic to a high degree. He was very down-to-earth, and had a talent for pulling the utmost effort out of the dancers. He was very exacting.

At home the dancers were often overworked. Rachel never had enough sleep. She describes rehearsing all afternoon and then walking to the one-room bed-sit which she shared with Elizabeth Woolen, a dancer in the company who had also come from New York. Their rooming house was on Assiniboine Avenue near the Assiniboine River, in a part of downtown Winnipeg where they could afford the rent on their paltry salaries. No buses ran to this part of town. The friends would rush to eat dinner at home and hike back through the sub-zero dark to the studio for night rehearsals.

Rachel remembers the shock of the cold. Often, she recalls, the ballerinas were required to be on pointe for many hours. She shudders to recall how torturous it was to put the pointe shoes back on cold feet for night rehearsals.

During the endless notes that followed rehearsals, Rachel would lie on the floor, spent. Sometimes, when the steam heat came hissing on, she fell asleep. Dancers who have worked with Rachel in later years are amazed by this admission. For when Rachel gives notes, she expects dancers to try them out right away. It would be unimaginable for anyone to fall asleep. In Rachel's ballerina days her naps could only have been a measure of complete exhaustion and the soporific effect of heat after cold.

Rachel yearned for the classic mode and this made up for a great many things about her situation in Winnipeg. Leaving New York, she had given up the notion of having a body ideal enough to dance in a major New York ballet company. She was resigned to the reality that she would not find roles in a large company where no one would know her dancing well enough to see and value her particular physical and dramatic talents.

Rachel had decided to stay on in Winnipeg after Harkarvy's departure, as she felt she had a fighting chance in this small, energetic company, something which a return to New York could not promise her. In fact, she says, dancing in Winnipeg made her raise her sights. The Royal Winnipeg Ballet, never a huge company, had only seventeen or eighteen dancers in those years. The company had always mounted many works, new and reconstructed. There were many roles for the hard-working dancers to tackle and many opportunities to perform. Rachel wanted to become a soloist and she did rise through the ranks of the Royal Winnipeg Ballet and dance as a soloist.

Friends told Rachel that she was well-suited temperamentally and physically to the contemporary work she performed with the ballet company. Rachel recalls her friend Marilyn Young saying, many years later, that she thought Rachel had a real feel for modern movement and that she could never understand why Rachel had persisted with ballet, as modern dance seemed such a good fit for her talents.

The only "barefoot ballet" Rachel was part of at the Royal Winnipeg was created for the company by American choreographer Robert Moulton, who came from Minneapolis, and was resident choreographer at the Tyrone Guthrie Theater. Called *Grasslands*, the work was set to music by Virgil Thompson titled *The Plough that Broke the Prairie*. The dance, created in 1958, had three sections, "Quilting Bee", "Saturday Night", and "Drouth". It took the company in a new and more contemporary direction than previous work. Rachel's recollection is that the work was considered daring. She recalls finding the movement quite natural. Its familiarity, in fact, felt too easy; she remained interested in the challenges of more classical work.

Robert Moulton was among the many young choreographers whose talent was recognized by Arnold Spohr. He received a number of invitations to work with the Royal Winnipeg Ballet. He danced with the company in 1959, performing a duet with a "prostitute" in *Grasslands*. He created two more works for the company, *Brave Song* (1959) and *The Beggar's Ballet* (1963). Later, his son Charlie Moulton was to dance in Rachel's company. Again, years after that, Charlie was to cause Rachel much pain through his renewed association with the Contemporary Dancers.

Eventually it became clear to Rachel that she would not be featured in the classics in Winnipeg. The company, always seeking to upgrade its reputation and the skills of the dancers, often brought in guest ballet mistresses and ballet masters. Rachel describes figuring out from the casting, after a couple of years with the company, that the ballet mistress at the time, Gwynne Ashton, whom Rachel recalls as a fantastic teacher and coach, had assessed her classical abilities and found her wanting. Nothing was ever said to Rachel, but the message was direct enough. She comforted herself with the thought that she had been a good enough dancer to be asked to stay on when Spohr became the director. "I had the spirit," says Rachel, "and the first cast had the body."

The season at the Royal Winnipeg Ballet was never more than about six months long. When other employment opportunities came along the dancers jumped at them. Rachel recalls working, first with Benjamin Harkarvy, later with Brian Macdonald, on a television series which took place in Winnipeg each spring for eight to twelve weeks. Producer Ernie Stagant wanted a different half-hour show each week. Rachel, who took part in these shows for three or four years, recalls that they chose a different theme each week. One week, for instance, they danced only to the music of Edvard Grieg.

Other summers Rachel was hired to take part in Rainbow Stage productions. One show she danced in was *Showboat*, which was choreographed by Spohr. She loved being outdoors and revelled in the opportunity to perform in the outdoor summer theatre.

Another production at Rainbow Stage was *The Pajama Game*, a musical theatre piece directed by John Hirsch. Hirsch, a founder of the Manitoba Theatre Centre, was considered a brilliant director and later became artistic director of the Stratford Festival. Because of her accent and her acting ability, Rachel became the understudy for Lillian Lewis, the actor playing the part of Adelaide in *The Pajama Game*. She attended Hirsch's rehearsals. She also attended drama classes with Hirsch for a year or two in the early 1960's at the Manitoba Theatre Centre. She remembers him liking her work on a Shakespearean monologue. Rachel flags these experiences with Hirsch as an important directoral influence. He was crazy and wild with enthusiasm; she found him an outstanding director.

Gweneth Lloyd and Betty Farrally, founders of the Royal Winnipeg Ballet, were gone by the time Rachel arrived in the company. However, she did dance in some of Lloyd's work and the legacy of the two was still strong in the company. Rachel remembers staying at Farrally's

Winnipeg house in River Heights one summer when she was doing seasonal work. She recalls Farrally packing a gang of young dancers into her little convertible on the Victoria Day weekend and driving like a fiend up to Grand Beach, an hour from Winnipeg. She has memories of how cold the lake was at the end of May, of getting sunburned and of loving the chance to get out of town. Farrally struck Rachel as very rough and ready, practical, if a too-fast driver.

Farrally was making a transition at the time, starting to teach in British Columbia. Rachel wonders how fully Farrally had moved on to her new life after leaving the Royal Winnipeg Ballet. Was she embittered? Was it distressing for her to watch this gaggle of carefree young dancers playing on the beach, full of enthusiasm, with opportunities for professional growth stretching out before them?

During Rachel's last full season with the company, her mother moved to Winnipeg. Rachel's father had died at the very end of the 1950's and Eva moved to be near her only daughter. She found some work as a caregiver for young children and as a companion to the elderly through the Jewish Child and Family Service.

Although Rachel loved the ballet, she was beginning to grow restive. In her mid-twenties, she was already feeling the passage of time. Her father's death brought home a sense of transition as well. Rachel was unsure whether she would achieve her cherished goals before she was too old to dance major classical roles. She knew that no matter how hard she worked technically, her penché would only go so high.

Rachel's career as a ballerina was to have interesting repercussions for the future. She was in a touring company, a small company, immersed in the ideas of programming the Royal Winnipeg Ballet had continued since its earliest days. The ongoing legacy of the company's feisty women founders was a blend of programming which stretched to embrace both ballet and contemporary sensibilities. During her years in the ballet, Rachel was carrying out this work with sweat and determination. Dreaming, eating, sleeping the work of the company and the dances she danced. Although Contemporary Dancers and Royal Winnipeg

Ballet are and always have been completely separate entities, being in this setting would at some level inform Rachel's ideas about shaping her own company.

But Rachel was caught, for a time, by conflicts in her own life and circumstances.

Motherhood and Teaching

In 1961, Rachel left the Royal Winnipeg Ballet.

"I left the ballet company which I dearly loved. I was a fanatic, I fanatically loved to perform and dance. I was a total bunhead ballet dancer. I just wanted to get up on stage in my pointe shoes and do classical ballet, and the more classical it was and the more difficult it was, the better I thought it was and the more challenge I felt."

Rachel attributes her decision to leave the company to her naiveté and to the prevailing social mores. She also felt it was time to reconsider, as she had realized that she was not going to rise to classical stardom. Ballet was a sport of the young. Rachel had it in the back of her mind that she would dance until her mid-to-late twenties, "old" for a dancer, and then start her family. "I was already," she recalls, "very influenced by a sick ballet mentality which stated that twenty-six is really old…"

She recalls, with some bitterness, her domestic situation around the time of her departure from the ballet. Her husband Don Browne had moved to Winnipeg in the months after she joined the Royal Winnipeg Ballet. He had become disillusioned with political realities in the United States and was looking for new horizons. It must have been a strain for them in those first years, as Rachel was away on tour for such long stretches of time.

Rachel was socialized, she says, to believe that part of being a "whole woman" was to have children. Her husband believed in the ideals of the nuclear family. In accord with their social ideals, the Brownes adopted their first daughter. Rachel remembers being convinced by Don to go ahead with the adoption. Once she was holding baby Ruth, she felt that it was a very poor choice to try to go on working with the ballet.

She could not imagine how she could cope with going on tour. So she resigned.

Women of twenty-six were supposed to stay home with their children and be happy homemakers. Rachel tried. Suddenly, she was at home all day with a child. She was abruptly and completely isolated from her identity as a dancer and from her life with the company, things for which she had worked long and hard. Rachel's feminism was not really fledged yet. Miserable, she tried her best to fit the role of the mother and homemaker.

In truth, all she wanted to do was to be involved with dance, to perform, to feel the pulse of a connection with a performing company. Rachel still practiced obsessively, willing herself through her barre in the kitchen, going to company classes and watching rehearsals, determined not to let her dancer's skills slip away.

"There I was with this adorable child and I did not want to be at home, not at all. I continued to practice fanatically and take every opportunity to attend classes with the company," recalls Rachel. "I was occupied with trying to dance and work on my technique even though I was in the house and it was very isolated. I was very, very unhappy. But at one level I was very happy. I remember taking my little girl, little Ruthie, to the park and teaching her how to walk holding my arms..."

Ironically, it was not until 1962, after Rachel had left the company, that Agnes de Mille came to work with the Royal Winnipeg Ballet. Working with her might have given a nudge to Rachel's devotion to the classical ideal of the ballerina. De Mille's writing had influenced Rachel as a teenager; the articulate choreographer might have become a mentor. Rachel did attend some of de Mille's rehearsals with the company.

Working with the Royal Winnipeg Ballet was an unexpectedly agreeable surprise to de Mille. She had come from New York City, in a skeptical frame of mind, to what must have seemed to her like the furthest reaches of civilization, to set *The Bitter Weird*. This was a dramatic "Scottish" ballet which used music from *Brigadoon*. De Mille set the work, featuring Richard Rutherford and Marilyn Young, whom she noted as a great dramatic dancer, as The Maiden. Then she went back to New York. When de Mille came back for the premiere she was mightily pleased by the way the company had "refined and clarified" her work. She was to return a number of times to work with the company.

Watching de Mille's rehearsals was agony for Rachel. "I believe the first dance de Mille did for the company was *The Bitter Weird*," she recalls. "My mouth would water when I would see this dance and I felt so abandoned. I felt as if I were not really human, as if I didn't have arms and legs, being at home."

Through these early family years she and Don adopted another girl, their middle daughter Miriam. And then, quite soon, Rachel was pregnant, and they had a third daughter Annette. Ruth, Miriam and Annette.

Rachel is still troubled about her early years of motherhood. Nurturing young children while staking a territory for personal growth is virtually impossible. The demands of raising her children made keeping her career alive a profoundly difficult and uneasy task for Rachel. She felt quite desperate.

"I always continued to practice even after we adopted the second child and I was very pregnant with my third daughter Annette. I was practising every day. I was practising the day I gave birth. And after...when I was in the hospital, I was doing my exercises immediately, because I was a fanatic...I had this absolute determination to keep my body in shape, to be able to perform, to not miss out on this thing that I desired so much..."

Faye Thomson, a co-director of the School of Contemporary Dancers, was a student at the Royal Winnipeg Ballet school as a child. She remembers seeing Rachel come in to take her class following Annette's birth. Though Thomson was quite young, she was struck by the force of Rachel's devotion. She recalls her intense focus; she recognized that Rachel was willing herself back into shape for dancing.

Rachel's daughters recall her iron will about her discipline at home. From ten to twelve in the mornings, while she was at home with them, she would take the telephone off the hook and practice. Her daughters remember that they were not permitted to interrupt. Anyone who has been at home with small children can sympathize, considering such conflicting claims.

After a time, Rachel began to teach. "I just grabbed the opportunity," she says, "because this was a chance to get out of the house and stay connected to dance. I loved and still love my kids very much," she goes on, "but I was very, very dissatisfied being home and I simply did not stay home. I found reasons and ways of getting out of the house."

Rachel started teaching at the Nenad and Jill Lhotka Ballet Studio. She knew the Lhotkas from their association with the Royal Winnipeg Ballet. Nenad had set *The Devil in the Village*, a folk-ballet based on Czech stories, for the Royal Winnipeg Ballet in 1956 and later returned to choreograph for the company in the mid-1960's when he made *Slaveni*. A Yugoslav dancer, he had worked as a ballet dancer in Zagreb for a decade before emigrating to Canada. He had been ballet master at the Royal Winnipeg Ballet for years until Ruthanna Boris' tenure ended that relationship. When Boris left the company Lhotka was offered the directorship, but declined it. His own school was consuming his energies by then.

The Lhotka Ballet Studio was in a large studio in the old Aragon Building at the corner of Smith Street and Graham Avenue in downtown Winnipeg. Although launching a career as a teacher was a new venture for Rachel, she had been coaching dancer friends since her New York days. Her self-confidence came to the fore. She knew she had the analytical ability to be a good teacher. She channelled her talents into the Lhotkas' school.

While Rachel's mother continued to live on her own, she began to help her daughter more and more with the children. Rachel looked after her children during the day and then went off to teach while her mother cared for them. "Mother stayed with the children, first with one, then with two, then with three. I was home all during the day. Classes started around five and I spent the whole evening and night at the Ballet Studio. Mother would come and do all the things I didn't do, cleaning, making meals—she was just completely selfless."

Rachel's children sometimes went with her when she went out to teach. Her eldest daughter Ruth has a memory of spending time, what felt like hours to her, parked in the corner of a studio in her snowsuit. She remembers some of the women at the studio were not very happy, with their mismatched legwarmers, coffee and cigarettes, stretching legs pushed open against a wall.

Soon after Rachel started teaching, a recital was scheduled at the Lhotka Ballet Studio. There was a need for more dances to fill out the concert program. Rachel took this need as a challenge and decided to try her hand at making dances for the senior students. She recalls using Brahms' waltzes to accompany her work. Making these dances for the ballet students whetted her appetite for choreography. She was hungry to be back on a stage again, hungry to dance again.

The time at the Lhotka Studio was significant to Rachel. Though she felt continually pulled by the needs of her family, though her level of dance activity seemed excruciatingly small, though the ache of not performing ate at her, change was incipient. This period of transformation was part of Rachel's growing away from ballet and into a whole new way of thinking about dance.

One quandary she fought was her loyalty to her own training. Her ballet background embodied formal ideals. Classical ballet is highly rigorous and explicit. Perfection of line, perfection of movement and musicality characterize its ideals.

Rachel's exposure to modern dance had been limited to her experiences with the Ryder-Frankel company in New York and performing Robert Moulton's *Grasslands* in Winnipeg. But the sensibility must have been working on her at some subtle level. Despite her expressed disinterest in modern dance, her choreography took a surprising turn.

Rachel recalls creating her first contemporary choreography. "I happened to be listening to some music by Odetta, southern folk songs and some spirituals and the music was just out of this world. I just started to move around to this music. I thought, I'll choreograph something, maybe for myself, and Nenad and Jill—they were very good dancers—and maybe I'll use them, and maybe we'll perform."

Odetta's Songs and Dances emerged, ingenuous, uncontrived dance. From this humble beginning Rachel's choreographic career was born.

"When this first dance came out of my body," she says, it certainly was not balletic... I had broken that strong connection to ballet because the movement looked, felt, contemporary, not balletic. It was just from inside, from my gut someplace... Many years later, copying some very old tapes of Contemporary Dancers, I looked at this old choreography and thought to myself that some of my instincts were really right on...It was very naive, primitive-looking choreography. But a lot of what I do today was there, in that early dance."

CONTEMPORARY DANCERS
—THE BEGINNING

Rachel created a few other dances besides *Odetta's Songs and Dances,* including *Turmoil,* which she set to a piece of music by Béla Bartók. The time seemed ripe for new dance activity in Winnipeg. Rachel, the Lhotkas and a group of young dancers gathered to perform. Effortlessly, they started to rise on the local scene. With typical plain-spokenness, Rachel called the company "Contemporary Dancers".

The company marked its official beginning in February, 1964, with an inaugural performance at the University of Manitoba. Contemporary Dancers shared a program with a musical group, the Marta Hidy Trio. Rachel recalls dancing "Greensleeves", a duet from *Odetta's Songs and Dances,* with Nenad Lhotka on this program. She was accustomed to dancing with the classical look of a bun. For this duet she decided to wear her hair loose, but soaked it to keep it down. Nenad Lhotka spent the dance dodging flying spray and Rachel's whipped, wet hair.

After the group's first appearance, invitations to perform followed from United College and the old Normal School or teachers' college. The new dance company started to blossom, giving numerous performances in its first and second years.

Rachel's daughter Annette Browne says that she was virtually born with the company. She grew up with Contemporary Dancers. In December, 1998 she marked her own birthday during the company's 35th anniversary celebrations.

Although the Royal Winnipeg Ballet and Contemporary Dancers are entirely separate, their histories contain interesting parallels in terms of the lines of support for cultural entities in the city. The Ballet always had ties of support from the University of Manitoba, drawing on administrative and design skills from the School of Architecture and other faculty. As well, it was one of the first ballet companies to receive a grant from the Canada Council, while Contemporary Dancers was the first modern dance company in the country to receive Council support.

⁂

Stephanie Ballard, choreographer and dancer, was an important figure in the growth and development of Contemporary Dancers. She remarks that change seems to be closely linked with extreme difficulty in Rachel's life. Change, when it comes for Rachel, is radical and fast. Newly fired with the conviction that she needed to study modern dance, Rachel charged off to pursue new training, leaving her pointe shoes at home.

She began to make yearly trips to New York to study the modern dance technique she needed to understand. She started to reverse her training and her whole way of thinking about dance. Her aesthetic shifted. She lost the exclusive dedication to "tippy-toe classical" dancing which had motivated her since early childhood.

She studied Graham technique intensely, then Limón and Cunningham, informing herself about all the major American modern dance styles. Rachel was finding a vocabulary and teaching philosophy which she has continued to evolve. She particularly loved the depth of movement of the Graham vocabulary. Through her study of Graham she started to love "heavy, rough, floor-bound" movement. The philosophy and movement qualities of Limón technique, having to do with weight, fall and recovery in the body, also suited her temperament and her physicality. She cites Ruth Currier, an original Limón company member and noted teacher of Limón technique, as an important influence in her deepening understanding of the modern idiom.

To this day Rachel makes excursions to New York to observe performances, classes and dancers. For years she travelled to New York to find dancers for her company. As the dance community in Canada started to grow and mature, skilled dancers began to graduate from the professional program of Contemporary Dancers' school, as well as from studios and schools in Vancouver, Toronto and Montreal. The new dance programs at York University and Simon Fraser University were to become sources of dancers for her company. But in those early years she often found dancers, especially male dancers, in the United States.

Rachel was eager to learn. She soaked up knowledge from her study trips to New York and summer programs. She was addressing a need larger than her own. She knew that she would bring back new expertise and new principles to pass on to the young dancers with whom she was working. She made contact with choreographers and teachers whom she invited to Winnipeg and absorbed new information from these guests.

Although she had no clear design in mind for the evolution of Contemporary Dancers, Rachel's ambition and her sense of responsibility were keen from the beginning. "She had a vigour and an urgency," recalls Faye Thomson, "that needed to burst out."

This state of brave and fearless naiveté as a starting point seems essentially different from Canadian dance culture now. Rachel started the company because finding a way to dance was imperative for her. There was no careful strategizing, no three- or five-year plan, no consultation with experts from other disciplines or countries, no corporate fundraising strategy. No government agencies to report to, not then, in any case.

And no job descriptions. She just started. What drove Rachel, and the growth and change of her company, was her own desire to achieve. Her sense of responsibility quickly expanded to embrace all the dancers in the burgeoning company. A wonderful, bullheaded, instinctive strength fired her. The prairie air, perhaps, started to steel her resolve. The company, in its first years, was a responsive and organic entity. Keeping her balance in times of change has been a paradox for Rachel, one of a handful who helped create a climate and culture for the shape-shifting art of contemporary dance in Canada.

In the company's earliest years, she did everything. She taught classes, hired dancers, organized and planned tours, did fundraising, created publicity materials, choreographed, and danced herself. Caught up in it, for a time Rachel somehow continued to harmonize the needs of her family, her budding company and her own artistic needs. But it was very difficult.

       ⁊   ⁊   ⁊

Rachel's marriage to Don Browne ended painfully. She had always felt that her first love was dance. Ideals of fulfilment within the nuclear family eroded as Rachel's insistent need to pursue her art fed her husband's growing dissatisfaction.

Considering why the relationship foundered, Rachel muses, "Don was generally very, very supportive and very knowledgable and very nice. He was a real generous guy, and he was very helpful, not just to me but to others too. At first I think I looked up to him as a father figure, someone with good ideas who I could listen to… It was much later, when I learned enough myself to know that I wanted not to listen to somebody else, that problems started."

When a split seemed inevitable, Rachel recalls that her gut instinct was to keep her children and her mother with her. Don convinced her otherwise. "My instinct," she recalls, "was to just take the three children. My mother and me and the three children. I didn't know how I would manage, but that's what I intended to do. Don convinced me otherwise. He begged to keep the two adopted children." Rachel must have been worried sick about how she could realistically hope to provide for her growing family. She was very vulnerable financially.

Rachel left. Very quickly after that, Don went to a lawyer and got an official separation agreement. Custody of Ruth and Miriam was given to her ex-husband and Rachel's visiting rights were severely restricted. By court order, she was allowed to see Ruth and Miriam only once during the week and every other weekend. She felt betrayed and torn from the two little girls, whom she loved dearly.

"I earned a little money teaching at the Lhotka Ballet Studio and I used to teach a few classes at the University of Winnipeg theatre department and at Tech. Voc. High School. But I lived on next to nothing… I got almost zero in terms of support from my ex-husband."

Rachel's mother continued to help her. Mother and daughter shared money for food and just managed to have enough to eat. Eva kept her own apartment. She lived in a tiny third-floor apartment which was, she said, "Cold in winter, but warm in the summer." She lived close to the inexpensive north end apartment which was Rachel's home for fourteen or fifteen years.

Both Eva and Rachel lived on practically nothing. But during these poor years, Rachel says, she never thought of going on welfare, because there was always a little bit of money. Whatever money she did make went toward expenses of her new company.

As a child, Alana Shewchuk, now a dancer with Winnipeg's Contemporary Dancers, was a student at the same dance school as Annette. She recalls that all the girls knew Rachel's mother. A familiar figure, a "teeny-weeny, little old lady", used to drop Annette off to her ballet lessons and come to collect her.

Rachel taught Annette "Sweet Potatoes", one of the sections of *Odetta's Songs and Dances*, when she was tiny. Annette was very shy, says her mother, but knew she did the dance very well and would agree to perform it for guests in their home. Rachel found her little daughter's dancing entirely charming. Annette remembers doing "Sweet Potatoes" while her granny watched indulgently. She remembers how she and her mother would practice together.

Without Eva's help looking after Annette, Rachel says, she could not have done the things she did. She could not have kept teaching or started to tour. She feels a great debt to her mother and is grateful for the way in which her mother allowed her to be the artist she needed to be. Though distraught about her family life, Rachel continued her dance life, teaching and working with her young company.

For several years, though, she lived with an acute sense of the loss of her daughters. Some of her acquaintances stopped speaking to her, as they felt she should have kept her family together. She was mournful, for she adored her girls. And she was angry at being so wilfully deprived of their company and of her presence in their lives. She never stopped trying to see Ruth and Miriam. "I broke the law," she remembers with bitter resentment. "I snuck around and found every way to see them."

As time went by her family's wounds would begin to heal. It became easier for them to spend time together; when the older girls became young teenagers, they could voluntarily choose to be with Rachel. And they had always holidayed together. Rachel always managed to scrape together enough money to get away with them. She describes hoarding her dollars, saving just enough to get on a bus and take her family to Florida, to stay in a cheap place by the shore.

The girls often accompanied Rachel when she went out of town to teach during the summers. In the late 1960's and early 1970's she did this regularly, making a bit of money and spreading the word about her company. Miriam recalls a photograph of Rachel and Annette, four or five years old, at a summer school in Nelson, British Columbia. The photograph is of mother and daughter in a dance class. Rachel was teaching, while Annette wandered out into the thick of things and stood in the middle of the class. Rachel's daughters remember this as a typical moment. In a way it might have been inappropriate for Annette to be in the grown-up dance setting, but no one really minded.

Rachel found every way she could to extend her summer trips with her daughters. These times of travelling and living with them were precious to her. She recalls one summer stopping off at the Banff Hot Springs with them. Another time, she let the older ones, by then young teenagers, get their ears pierced. This indulgence got Rachel into hot water with their father when the girls' ears became badly infected back in Winnipeg.

Balancing, groping, juggling, searching. Rachel has known hard times and the loneliness that often accompanies commitment to a goal or an art. What sustained her was the dance. Always. Colleagues and friends who have known her a long time call dance the real partner in her life. She says it herself.

"My focus during all this time, the marriage, the children, the divorce, the separation, was always chiefly on the dance."

There was no support for the growing company's activities from the Canada Council for several years. When assistance came, it was in the form of support for Rachel's growth as an individual artist. The Canada Council expressed their confirmation of Rachel's excellence as a dancer.

They felt that encouraging her development through continuing study was a good investment, as she would use her deepening understanding to develop the dancers in her young company.

As Contemporary Dancers' artistic director, Rachel's relationship with the Canada Council was never an easy one. She recalls being personally awarded an "Arts Grant A", a senior level grant of $25,000, while the company received only $6,000 in support. Her manager at the time, Bob Holloway, insisted that she plough the money she received into the company account.

"I remember feeling very resentful about the fact that Canada Council assessors were always very, very complimentary about my dancing. They felt that it had substance, strength, originality, maturity, and I always felt very bad that I got all the good assessments...The dancers, they said, were still young, and rather juvenile and undeveloped and they needed more modern technique."

Rachel was recognized as the defining note of the quality of the company, her dancing and choreography central to its identity. Early Council comments also pointed out that Rachel's choreography for herself was very substantive, while her choreography for the company ensemble tended to be light or entertaining by comparison.

Rachel was very young as a director, but as she gained in experience her confidence about whom to hire and how to train dancers grew rapidly. She did know that she wanted to please audiences as well as challenge them. She knew that if she showed only serious, difficult dance, her audience would dry up. This influenced her programming choices in the company's early days.

Rachel felt that she needed to offer her audiences a diversity of styles and artistic points of view in her programming. In the mid-to-late 1960's there were no funded single-choreographer companies. That did not upset her as she did not want the responsibility of programming whole evenings of Rachel Browne. She felt that she did not have the huge choreographic talent which could sustain entire programs. And she wanted to continue to dance herself. It was consistent with her humanist ideals to offer a breadth of approaches both to the company and to her audiences.

For many reasons, a certain kind of artistic compromise for Rachel was built right into the beginning of Contemporary Dancers' activities. This is a familiar quandary for people who have immediate creative needs within a larger circumstance for which they are responsible. Complications can rise from the genuine and generous desire to build a large context and from the impulse to benefit and nurture younger artists. Ironically, compromise of one's real artistic path can come through the need to defend one's explorations in such a large context, which soon grows to address many artistic needs. These issues often seem to plague women, certainly the first movers of dance. Rachel took it all on.

꙳   ꙳   ꙳

Rachel says she never thought of the future, she just wanted to dance. Yet she was also very enterprising when she saw that there were opportunities to be cultivated. She enthusiastically started making contacts, finding occasions for the company to be seen locally.

Contemporary Dancers gave a number of performances in Winnipeg in the first half of 1965. In February they appeared at the University of Manitoba. In March the company performed for students at United College and gave performances at the Manitoba Teachers' College. They also gave four performances at the Manitoba Theatre Centre Across the Street Theatre. In July of that first season, they appeared on a half-hour CBC show called "Across the Nation". They presented selections from the company's repertory.

During its second year, the 1965-66 season, the company's activities expanded in a way that was very satisfying to Rachel. With eight dancers, six women including Rachel and two male dancers, the company started its season with October performances at United College. Later that month they appeared in Kenora, Ontario. In November they returned to the University of Manitoba and in January of 1966 travelled to Brandon, Manitoba. In January and again in May, 1966 they went to Fort William, Ontario. In April the company gave four performances at the Manitoba Theatre Centre Across the Street Theatre. During this season Contemporary Dancers also began to tour in schools, giving seven lecture-demonstrations in junior high schools in the Winnipeg area.

Writer Michael Olver reviewed the company's spring season for the *Winnipeg Tribune* on April 7, 1966. Although he seemed alternately bemused by the choreography and smitten with the beauty of the young dancers, he noted that the theatre was packed for the company's final program of the season. He commented, "Mrs. Browne and her dancers, Jill Alis, Marilyn Lewis, Cheryl Belkin, Jennifer Ingram, Barbara Barsky and Cherie Smith, are trying to do the unusual, but they are not, I am sure, doing it just to shock. Their dancing and the whole style of their production has too much integrity. If they err, it is on the side of over- statement: but time, more work together and a continuing and sympathetic audience should cure that."

Contemporary Dancers began to tour about two years before as- sistance from grants started to come. Rachel knew that she needed to provide at least six months' work each year in order to keep her dancers dancing. Touring is synonymous with employment for dancers in Win- nipeg. So Rachel picked up the telephone to act as a tour booker for the company.

By its third season, the company travelled to Atikokan, Ontario, returned to Fort William, and gave a performance in Souris, Manitoba. In Winnipeg they danced at the Manitoba Theatre Centre, the YMHA, two synagogues, and United College. They also appeared on the televi- sion show "Century West" and appeared at a noon-time "Music on Campus" concert at the University of Winnipeg. As well, Contempo- rary Dancers gave fifteen lecture-demonstrations in junior high and high schools in Winnipeg. In 1967, Rachel was awarded her first grant from the Canada Council.

A May, 1967 series of spring performances featured five works. Four of these were made by Rachel. Included on this program were *Odetta's Songs and Dances* (1964), the premieres of *Anerca* (1967) and *Pas le Même Pas* (1967), a work built on jazz and bossa nova rhythms, and *Evening in the Suburbs*, a 1966 work which used poetry by Raymond Souster and an original score by Victor Davies. Also on the program was *Visions Fugitives*, which Rachel had commissioned from Nenad Lhotka in 1965. Set to music by Sergei Prokofiev, *Visions* received very good notices. A local newspaper review of May 13, 1967, written by Michael Kostelnuk, described it as modern dance of the best kind, able to show compelling truths about human motivation through the essence of movement.

Rachel's new choreography *Anerca* was inspired by the North. Supported by a grant from the Manitoba Centennial Corporation, *Anerca* was the company's contribution to Canada's centennial celebrations. The program note read, "Based on traditional Eskimo songs and chants and set to a complementary electronic score, *Anerca* translates a remote Canadian culture into universal terms. Traditional patterns and abstract movements recreate the timeless life cycle of the Eskimo."

In July, Contemporary Dancers travelled to Montreal to give seven performances in the Festival of the Arts at Expo '67. The eight women in the company, including Rachel, performed on an outdoor stage without benefit of lights, curtain or wings. They had a short performance time and Rachel chose to show a "sampler" of the works that the company was dancing at the time, including excerpts of *Anerca*, *Pas le Même Pas* and *Songs and Dances*.

By the 1968-69 season, Rachel had successfully captured a spot in the cultural life of Winnipeg for her young dance troupe. The company's spring season was given in the Manitoba Theatre Centre on April 26 and 27, 1968. The program notes that both Robert Moulton's *Rondo ad Absurdum* and Rachel's *Miles Smiles*, described in the program as an "uptempo jazz fantasy", premiered in these performances. The performances were also historically significant. As Rachel noted, "This program will mark the last public performance at M.T.C. before the theatre is demolished. Contemporary Dancers extends a wistful farewell to a theatre that has served its community so well."

Though it was still an amateur local company, Rachel was building Contemporary Dancers' strength and reputation. She made the best of her local contacts. Early on she worked with Nenad Lhotka. Arnold Spohr, a friend from Rachel's Royal Winnipeg Ballet days, occasionally came in to watch rehearsals. He helped to facilitate Rachel's commissioning of choreographer James Clouser, who was a principal dancer, rehearsal director and choreographer with the Royal Winnipeg Ballet. Once or twice Rachel "borrowed" male dancers, notably Richard Browne, from the ballet. Choreographer Robert Moulton was a significant contributor to Contemporary Dancers' early repertory. Perhaps the model of the Royal Winnipeg Ballet encouraged Rachel's boldness; the ballet company had always looked to outside sources for teaching and choreographic inspiration, as well as cultivating "homegrown" talent.

In its fourth season Contemporary Dancers appeared at all the city's major cultural venues, including the Winnipeg Art Gallery, Playhouse

Theatre, University of Manitoba and University of Winnipeg. They gave four performances in Winnipeg Symphony Youth concerts and fifteen lecture-demonstrations in junior and senior high schools. In February of 1969 the company completed a half-hour CBC show. Directed by Don Williams, it featured works from the company's repertory. The dancers gave about a dozen performances on tour, including appearances in Pinawa, Manitoba, in Port Arthur and Dryden in northern Ontario, and in Calgary, Edmonton, Regina and Prince Albert, Saskatchewan. They also stepped over the border to appear in Bottineau, North Dakota at an international music camp and at the North Dakota State School of Science in Wahpeton.

Justifiably proud of these achievements, in a late 1960's brochure Rachel described the company as

"Winnipeg's professional modern dance company, a compact, versatile touring attraction of eight.
Now Available For Bookings"

Deborah Lundmark was a seventeen-year-old dance student in Saskatoon when she first auditioned for Contemporary Dancers. Rachel travelled to Saskatoon in 1968 to hold auditions. There was no other modern dance company in Western Canada at that time. Rachel was it, as far as the young Saskatoon dancers knew. Lundmark was desperate to be chosen for Contemporary Dancers. Rachel gently encouraged her to go on with her training. Lundmark continued to show up every year until 1975 at Rachel's auditions in Saskatoon, and later in Toronto. By chance she met Rachel at the airport the first year she did not audition. Rachel rushed up to her exclaiming, "Deborah, where were you? You might have made it this year!"

Dance travels like dandelions, patches of furious activity often sprouting from a single blown seed. The vision of contemporary dance which Rachel carried to Saskatoon in the late 1960's has had far-reaching effects. Though Lundmark never did dance with Contemporary Dancers, Rachel's wisdom, kindness and attentiveness as a director, teacher and choreographer have continued to be a model for her ideals of teaching and directing her own company, Toronto's Canadian Children's Dance Theatre.

⟩   ⟩   ⟩

A tour during the 1969-70 season took the company on an extended circuit through Manitoba and Saskatchewan schools. The dancers travelled in one car with a station wagon which carried sound and lighting equipment. They did two and often three shows a day. Sometimes they were in a theatre; most often they performed in school auditoriums. Although they reached hundreds of students through these performances, they did not have any other contact with the children. There was no class or workshop time scheduled, as this touring predated the popularity of study guides.

Rachel recalls the first time she ever saw the harvest moon riding the sky over the Saskatchewan prairie. She did love the travelling, although she found being the boss on tour an isolating job. She did not enjoy the fact that she always had to be the "bad guy", arranging rehearsal spaces, drawing up the schedule, prodding the dancers to make sure the company left on time for its next appearance.

But Rachel was still dancing and loving it. It fired her desire to stay enmeshed in dance. Without the pleasure and reward of this deep joy, she says, she might have left. Her love of dance sustained her through these first hard and lonely experiences of being a director.

When she got fed up being lonely, when her still-married friends forgot to include her in their social activities, she took the initiative. She stopped feeling offended. If she was feeling a need for company and was without a man in her life, she would call friends and just invite herself over. She did meet some people in this way, and felt it was appropriate for her to initiate relationships. A number of men were offended by such behaviour, but others, she reflects, seemed flattered by her directness.

"These years of being on my own did teach me a great deal. They taught me a lot about how to make my own happiness happen and how to be self-sufficient and how to live on next to nothing."

Rachel muses that she must have had a sense that Contemporary Dancers would survive and expand. She set herself to finding members for the first board of directors. She began to look for ways to fund-raise. She began to think in a long-term way about building a repertory of dances and about venues and opportunities for the company. She began to think about the responsibility of training dancers. She began to consider how to find the right dancers for her own choreographic intentions and for the other choreography she was acquiring for the company. She began to find ways to get people to help her with essential tasks such as making and ironing costumes. She began to concern herself with how to make audio tapes, where to store tapes and costumes, and how to beg or steal adequate rehearsal time.

All this time Rachel was trying to keep enough food on the table. She was still teaching ballet and beginning to teach modern dance at the Lhotka Studio, as well as at the University of Winnipeg. A typewritten information sheet which she prepared about the company, dated May 8, 1969, lists her teaching accomplishments to that time.

"1. dance therapist, 3 yrs., Kinsmen School for Retarded, Wpg. Psychiatric Inst.
2. on staff at the M.T.C. theatre school-4 yrs.
3. on staff at the Lhotka Ballet Studio-8 yrs.
4. on staff in the Theatre and Broadcasting Dept., Tech.Voc. High School
5. 69/70 School Terms-instructor, Drama Dept., Univ. of Wpg.
6. conducted numerous workshops at the Univ. of Man., the Univ. of Alberta, and in most of the centres mentioned above, in the list of recent performances."

This information sheet also describes Contemporary Dancers as a "modern dance co. whose most important function is to bring high quality dance to uninitiated audiences." Rachel goes on to say that, "Each of the dancers is thoroughly trained in ballet, modern and jazz techniques in order to meet the demands of the varied repertoire, which includes lighter jazz, folk, and humourous works, as well as serious dramatic works, and experimental projects with dances set to electronic scores and 'now' music."

Rachel's daughters remember her always being on the telephone, pressing forward without assistance. Rachel remembers working eighteen- or twenty-hour days. Miriam recalls her mother having to fight for her aims and beliefs, having to advocate vigourously for herself in every way.

"She didn't have a general manager or an assistant or theatre support," recalls Miriam. "She was it. Fundraising calls, typing up her programs, creating her audiences...everything."

CONTEMPORARY DANCERS
— EARLY YEARS AND THE SCHOOL

Rachel was to need her toughness and self-sufficiency. Her resilience was tested again and again through her company. Throughout her years as Contemporary Dancers' artistic director, she had a particularly rough ride with management. Her experience has been shared by many, for managers and artists rarely stay happily married for long. Ideally, a manager's love for dance makes the art a priority in all considerations. This level of commitment to the art is exceedingly rare.

Contemporary Dancers' first grants and first manager arrived at roughly the same time. Bob Holloway started working with the company in 1970. He had a background working in publicity with the Royal Winnipeg Ballet. Stephanie Ballard, who joined the company soon after Holloway's arrival, remembers him as important in helping Rachel build the company.

Rachel was relieved to share her workload. Holloway was an expert in promotion and created impressive materials for the company's use. Rachel describes his projection of the company's image as "slick", while at the same time handsome and effective. People remarked to Rachel how fine they were, even in the days when the company was just getting off the ground artistically.

Holloway's work with the company marked a time of change. By 1970 the company was in a position to offer its seven dancers a five-month contract. The company settled into its first studios in the historic Aragon building at the corner of Smith and Graham where Nenad and Jill Lhotka had their school. The building has since been torn down; Winnipeg's Centennial Library was built on the site. Contemporary Dancers took over what had been the Aragon Ballroom, a huge space with a wonderful wooden floor and a mirror ball, relic of wartime dances and nights of big band magic. Scores of pigeons lived inside the studio, nesting high up in the rafters.

There was also a second, smaller studio. Holloway, an enterprising man who "got things done", had office spaces built right into the ballroom. His initiative signified a new level of operations for Contemporary Dancers.

In the 1970 season the company became the first dance company to tour in the far North. A year or two earlier Rachel had arranged the tour to the Northwest Territories through a musical organization called Overture Concerts. Managed by George Zuckerman, the organization usually booked musical groups in smaller communities. Rachel recalls sensing that Overture Concerts viewed contracting Contemporary Dancers as an opportunity to make some money. No doubt the dance company's fees reflected this.

However, Rachel needed to keep her dancers working and this tour also offered a fascinating opportunity to see the far North. Travelling by plane, the company followed the musical touring circuit, journeying as far north as Inuvik. Quite quickly, Rachel realized that they were mostly dancing for civil servants. The company was booked into some residential schools as well. Wherever they performed a number of indigenous people would always come to see them, though it was obvious that they had no way to connect to the dancing the company presented. Rachel recalls native families offering the dancers moccasins and beaded cloth for sale.

Rachel speaks about performing her work *Anerca* in the North. She had no thought of creating an Inuit work. *Anerca* was a modern dance, costumed in a way reminiscent of traditional Inuit clothing. The costumes and set were by Taras Korol, a design artist of distinction. The colouration, Rachel says, came from the North. The dance was made in seven sections—"morning", "girls' dance", "hunt", "celebration", "hunger", "old song", and "dreams". The dance was accompanied by a collage of music from Edgar Varese, Tzvi Avni and Walter Carlos. Rachel danced the "old song" section of the work as a solo.

For Rachel, a highlight of this northern tour was seeing the Delta Drum Dancers. The group attended a performance by Contemporary Dancers and then performed in turn. All elders, the youngest members of the troupe were from sixty to sixty-five years old. They kept the

Inuit dance traditions alive. Rachel remembers being thrilled by the privilege of seeing them, understanding what an honour it was to see and hear these keepers of the dance.

Early in its development Contemporary Dancers started to bring in guest choreographers from out of town. Rachel always invited her choreographic guests to teach company classes. She did this in order to deepen her dancers' understanding of each choreographer's approach to movement, and to enrich the company's training. Initially, these were mostly people Rachel knew from New York. Robert Moulton was the first choreographic guest.

The company was quite daring in its first offerings. Rachel was brave in her choices of company visitors, but she was also thrifty. Even when she did not love the work which her guests created, she programmed it for a time, making the most of the company's investment of time and resources.

Stephanie Ballard arrived in Winnipeg in 1972. Originally from California, she felt an immediate rapport with Rachel, another dancer with a ballet background who came from the United States. She recalls Rachel as very warm, very demanding, and even to her untutored eye at the time, a fine dancer. Ballard recalls noticing that Rachel performed even in rehearsal.

Rachel invited Ballard to join the Contemporary Dancers' apprentice program, which was just beginning in 1972. Ballard remembers being astonished that her very first class was with James Waring, a quirky, innovative luminary of the New York avant-garde. In the mid-to-late 1960's, dance artists involved with New York City's Judson Church movement began to redefine dance and theatrical boundaries. An accomplished and celebrated choreographer, teacher and rethinker of dance, James Waring was among them.

He came from a ballet foundation, but invented movement and dance works in a style all his own. Waring, unlike any of his Judson Church colleagues, considered any work made for the theatrical stage a "ballet".

He created *Happy Ending* for the company, a work set to a Mozart piano concerto. Rachel recalls this piece with awe, remembering its beautiful construction. It moved wonderfully, with the simplest of movement. Rachel reflects that of the first wave of choreographers she brought into the company, Waring was perhaps the most strange and innovative. She recalls him asking for the dancers' astrological signs before beginning work with them. His work was very dramatic and theatrical; he expected the company dancers to work very hard.

While he was working with the company, Rachel asked Waring to make a solo for her. With an absurdist sense typical of the titles of his works, he called his piece for her *Rune to a Green Star*. The solo was set to the Debussy concerto for clarinet and orchestra. Rachel and Waring worked in the company's small second studio while making the dance. From its days as the Aragon Ballroom, the room still featured a bar with a sign hanging over it which read "Steamed Hot Dogs 5 cents". Her solo, which Rachel calls the most innovative choreography she did for many years, was performed widely on the company's tours. Although she says audiences didn't know what to make of it, she danced it with enjoyment. Waring's joke title for the dance was "Steamed Hot Dogs". Rachel once saw the dance called this in a program, after she taught the solo to Ze'eva Cohen, an acclaimed New York-based modern dancer. After Waring died, Rachel was asked to take part in a tribute to him. She danced his *Rune to a Green Star* to very favourable critical notice in New York.

In 1972, Sophie Maslow, a former Graham company member, set her dance *Country Music* for the company. In the 1972-73 season Contemporary Dancers performed New York-based Paul Sanasardo's *Metallics*. Sanasardo, recalls Rachel, was very well-regarded at that time; his work, though idiosyncratic and highly charged kinetically, was more conservative than James Waring's. The company also danced Waring's *Happy Ending* during this season and presented a work by American choreographer Norman Walker called *Three Psalms*, which included what the choreographer termed "controlled nudity". Rachel recalls the Winnipeg police taking a very close interest in the morality of this work in performance. The Winnipeg audience was very interested in *Three Psalms* too. Performances sold out.

According to archival research by Stephanie Ballard, during the 1972-73 season Contemporary Dancers logged 20,000 touring miles and gave one hundred and four performances.

Rachel was continuing to create new dances, though for several years her choreographic output was quite small. In 1969 she had choreographed a work she titled *Variations*, setting it to J.S. Bach's *Goldberg Variations*. This was one of the first works which Stephanie Ballard performed with the company. At the time Ballard joined Contemporary Dancers, Rachel was the company's main teacher, giving ballet and modern dance classes on alternate days. Ballard remembers putting on her pointe shoes in ballet class and being called on to dance on pointe in Rachel's *Variations*. Later, Rachel changed the look of this dance somewhat by having the dancers perform it in soft slippers and pantyhose, as Ballard recalls with a shudder, remembering the dancers' discomfort.

Ruth Asper and Miriam Browne recall going as children to see Contemporary Dancers at the Playhouse Theatre. Recently, their memories were stirred by seeing 1972 posters for the company displayed in the theatre lobby. As children going to watch Contemporary Dancers perform, they were very proud of their mother, though they did not always know quite what they were seeing.

Ruth says she likes to know what the story behind things is. She recalls being in the car, driving home after a performance one night, puzzled, pressing her mother with questions. "What was it about Mom? What was it about? What was the story?" Her child's mind was unable to comprehend what her mother meant when Rachel replied, "It's about dance." Or "It's about the music and space."

In 1973, Rachel and Bob Holloway began the School of Contemporary Dancers. It was started for practical reasons, as a way of generating income. As well, it was a means of spreading knowledge of contemporary dance in Winnipeg. The school had two components, a general school for the community, and more advanced instruction for aspiring dancers. The general school grew from its initial enrolment of about forty students to its peak size of about five hundred before the mid-1980's recession affected registration. In the mid-1990's the school's population stabilized between two and three hundred. From the beginning, Rachel's nurturing, possibly fed by memories of the early encouragement she received in her own music and dance lessons, cleared the way for very talented students who came through the professional part of the school. Many were provided with encouragement and training in preparation for professional careers.

The two present directors of the professional program came to Rachel's attention through the school and company. Faye Thomson, a teacher, became an apprentice with Contemporary Dancers at Rachel's invitation in 1973. After serving as the general school's first principal she became one of the professional program's co-directors. Thomson had a foundation as a ballet dancer and a decade-long performing career as an Indian classical dancer, as well as a dance degree from York University in Toronto.

Her partner in running the professional program is Odette Heyn-Penner. Initially she went to Winnipeg as an apprentice to Contemporary Dancers following dance studies at York University. Rachel invited her to become involved with Contemporary Dancers professional program.

At its inception the professional program was more of a junior company. Initially it was under the direction of Marian Sarach, who had danced with James Waring and with the Martha Graham company before her sojourn in Winnipeg. Guided by Sarach, members of this junior company did a substantial amount of performing. They took over some of Contemporary Dancers' local school touring while the "older" company concentrated more on concert appearances and on touring outside Winnipeg.

Later the professional program evolved to being a true apprentice program and was attached more directly to the company. Stephanie Ballard took on the responsibility of being the director of the apprentice program in 1979. Rachel asked Odette Heyn-Penner to assume responsibility as co-director of the professional program, joining Faye Thomson.

The School of Contemporary Dancers is at times referred to as "Canada's best-kept dance secret". Guided by Heyn-Penner and Thomson, the school has quietly flourished, training many future company members. It sustains an excellent reputation as a training ground for contemporary dancers in Canada. It is known as a centre of fine, careful teaching and is one of three acknowledged Canadian training centres for professional contemporary dancers, along with the School of Toronto Dance Theatre and Les Ateliers de Danse Moderne de Montreal (LADDMI).

Rachel's association with the school as a guide, teacher and choreographer has continued through good times and dreadful times in other areas of her professional life. Her relationship with the school is an unbroken cord.

Bob Holloway's years as manager of Contemporary Dancers were a period of expansion. Holloway was a skilled administrator, and was also very successful at booking the company. His administration marked the company's transition from amateur to professional status. Meanwhile, the company continued to expand artistically. For a time the two sets of aspirations for growth matched stride.

In 1971 Contemporary Dancers began a very successful subscription series. This built to the point where, at its peak in the mid-1970's, recalls Rachel, the company sold a thousand subscription memberships each season. This was highly unusual, a remarkable achievement for contemporary dance anywhere on the continent. The company performed at the Playhouse Theatre, making it the home of their Winnipeg seasons for five or six years. Contemporary Dancers filled the Playhouse/Pantages theatre downstairs, which had twenty-five hundred seats, without difficulty. As a rule they gave three Winnipeg seasons per year during this period. The company regularly undertook national tours and toured in the United States.

Rachel remembers how the company "used to travel across the country in an old yellow school bus which we had painted blue. The bus had very little heat and there was a space cleared out at the back for our lights and sound equipment..."

Rachel's programming was a large part of the company's success. She created equilibrium in programs of innovative and more traditional works, programs which had a broad appeal.

Early on, she had managed to find the means to commission work from Robert Moulton for Contemporary Dancers. The popularity of his work had impressed her at the Royal Winnipeg Ballet and she invited him to create a number of works for Contemporary Dancers. The first was *Rondo ad Absurdum* (1968), "a big hit" for the company, in which the dancers sported with flowers between their toes. Journalist Frank Morriss, writing for the *Winnipeg Free Press*, called the work, "An outrageously funny satire...an absolute tongue-in-cheek delight." *True Believer*, Moulton's next work for the company, made in 1969, was performed in silence. *Kinetics II*, set to music by Rodrigo, was acclaimed in the *Calgary Albertan* as "dancing with exuberance, the rites of love..." In 1970 Moulton made a work titled *Turn In, Turn Out, Turn On, or Bach is Beautiful*. A popular favourite and a key work in the company's repertory for several years, the dance was performed many times at home and on tour. In 1971 he created *Eight Rituals for Dancers*, which was programmed for Contemporary Dancers' January, 1974 performances.

Rachel contracted Richard Gain, a highly regarded New York-based choreographer with an intensely physical style, to give the company two works. These were on the program for their January, 1974 performances. *Fellow Voyager*, premiering in these performances, featured dancer William Holahan making his entrance by being lowered from the ceiling. Rachel recalls this as an intensely dramatic entrance. Gain's other work for Contemporary Dancers, mounted for the company in 1972, was titled *I Never Saw Another Butterfly*. It drew on images from a book of drawings made by children while they were imprisoned in Theresienstadt, a concentration camp in Czechoslovakia, during World War II. It was a controversial work, and long; Rachel recalls it requiring "courageous programming".

The company's season in March, 1974 featured Rachel's *Contrasts*, set to music by Béla Bartók, and *Gaspard et Rosina*, a work by Marian Sarach, who was Rachel's assistant director at that time. Rachel recalls her as a gifted choreographer, whose work for the company was often hilarious. Paul Sanasardo's *Metallics* and James Waring's solo for Rachel, *Rune to a Green Star,* were presented on these spring programs as well.

During the 1974-75 season, Contemporary Dancers toured for a month, travelling 10,000 miles to fifteen cities in the U.S., giving twenty performances on the tour. During this season, Marian Sarach continued to assist Rachel, now as a second artistic director for the company. Rachel remounted *Anerca*, presenting it in the company's season in October, 1974. Also on the program of these Winnipeg performances on October 25 and 26 were two works by Canadian choreographer Norbert Vesak, *First Century Garden* and *Angel Within*.

Rachel continued to cultivate choreographic talent close to home. In January, 1975, the company's season included a work by James Clouser, titled *Danses Sacres et Profonds*. Rachel collaborated with Marian Sarach on a choreography called *Pastoral*, which was presented in March, 1975 performances. Sarach made two other works with the company. One, titled *The Last Shimmy*, was set to Scott Joplin piano rags and was part of the company's autumn 1974 season. The other work, which she called *Saskatoon Pie*, was presented March 21 and 22, 1975.

Rachel is reflective about putting her choreographic career on the back burner during these first company years. She was ambitious for the company, and made many adventurous choices. The company reflected her aesthetic very strongly through her choice of guest choreographers. She aimed for ways of reaching and challenging large audiences.

On the surface, bringing in other artists seemed to be to the detriment of her own choreographic development. The company's creative resources were being used by artists other than Rachel. But her determination to keep on dancing herself fed this need to look outside.

In some ways too, Rachel's choreographic evolution is related to the different eras of guests she brought in. Without consciously meaning to, she was absorbing details about the creative process. Rachel was soaking up the influences of these skilled creators through watching their works come together, through rehearsing and occasionally dancing in their works, as well as through staging them.

Bob Holloway's association with the company lasted from 1970 to 1975. This was Rachel's first experience of dealing with management. Although she had built a successful career as a ballerina, navigated the tricky waters of ballet company dynamics, acquired skill as a choreographer and gone in new directions as a teacher, booking agent, organizer and fund-raiser for her company, Rachel remained a novice in terms of power within an organization.

Rachel recalls Holloway as capable and ambitious. She also recalls virtually handing power to him. Initially, she was immensely relieved to be divested of total responsibility for the company's activity, giving her more time to devote to the artistic part of her responsibilites, to classes, rehearsals, scheduling, coaching dancers and other claims on her attention.

Rachel recalls allowing Holloway, quite quickly after he started working with the company, to do most of the negotiating with the board of directors and funding agencies. The company started to expand its financial base, heading toward greater stability. Concurrent with this expanding picture, the relationship between management and artistic direction started to fray. She and Holloway had started out on quite a democratic footing, Rachel recalls. Holloway knew Rachel's salary and Rachel believed she knew his.

Winnipeg writer Melinda McCracken interviewed Bob Holloway in the mid-1980's, long after he had left Contemporary Dancers. It is Rachel's understanding, through what this interview revealed, that Holloway came to think that the company, once it gained momentum, would be better off replacing her.

"That's how I interpreted it, that he felt that I was at my best when the company was really struggling…but that when it was getting on its feet he felt I wasn't such a good artistic director and that maybe the company would fare better with a different artistic director, more objective, more skilled, less home-grown…which from a manager's point of view makes utter sense."

But, continues Rachel, the company had been born out of her need to perform and choreograph. Taking away the heart of the company would have destroyed it. Despite her growing uneasiness, Rachel went on, busy with her daily dance work, until the door to the company was implicitly shut in her face.

Holloway wanted to lock her out of the office. He wanted to prevent her having access to certain company files. Faced with this evidence that secrets were being kept from her, that information about the administration and about aspects of the future direction of the company was being held back, Rachel took action.

She went to the chair of her board of directors, Rosalie Goldstein, to protest these developments. Goldstein was a great supporter of Rachel's, and a believer in her achievements. At Goldstein's behest the board of directors let Holloway go in 1975. But the change did not occur until the situation had escalated to a point where Holloway was very angry and on the verge, it seemed, of manoeuvering Rachel out of the company. The board, at the end of his time with Contemporary Dancers, saw no alternative but to lock him out.

THE MIDDLE YEARS
—DANCING THROUGH THE 1970'S

A series of managers was to follow. Naomi Permit, David Williams and Janice Fontaine all managed the company for periods of time. Rachel remembers their years of administration as a cycle of ups and downs, in part because they were such pleasant human beings that they were not particularly effective managers.

Meanwhile, the company itself was bubbling along. In 1970 the company had hired seven dancers on a five-month contract. By comparison, in 1977, under the administrative direction of David Williams, Contemporary Dancers had grown to being able to offer twelve dancers a seven-month contract. By then the company had support from the Manitoba Arts Council and the City of Winnipeg, as well as from the Canada Council.

During the mid-1970's the company moved several times. When they had to leave the Aragon Ballroom and "Steamed Hot Dogs", Contemporary Dancers rented space from a theatre company, Prairie Theatre Exchange, in Winnipeg's historic Exchange District. After several years the company moved again, still within the Exchange District, this time to a building that was also occupied by the Manitoba Theatre for Young People. By the late 1970's, Contemporary Dancers moved into studios and offices in the Augustine United Church on Pulford Street, where the school and the company have remained since.

In some ways these changes were symbolic of the company's journey toward stability and a maturing identity. The company was healthy, growing, carving a niche nationally, and making its presence felt internationally.

Rachel continued to be ambitious for her company while

maintaining her ties with American modern dance. She continued to make trips to New York, taking class, looking at performances, negotiating with choreographers for the acquisition or creation of work, auditioning dancers. Contemporary Dancers was a significant commissioner of new choreography and remounted a good deal of existing work.

Rachel started to shift the company's creative focus in the mid-1970's. As dance bloomed elsewhere in the country, she began to look across Canada, rather than just to the United States, for commissioning possibilities. Judith Marcuse, a Canadian returning from the English company Ballet Rambert, was the first Canadian choreographer Rachel commissioned. Very quickly after that Contemporary Dancers became an important commissioner of budding Canadian choreographers. Rachel also hired Canadian choreographers to set already existing work for her company. Her programs began to represent a new blend of styles, aesthetics, ways of creating and mounting dance work.

In making *Domino*, choreographer Linda Rabin realized that although it allowed her creative latitude, a repertory company situation was not the best circumstance for the new line of development she felt compelled to follow. There were too many claims on the company's time, too many other dances to rehearse and pieces to be nurtured, too many inherent limitations about the length of work for a repertory program. So Rabin re-thought her creative needs, a process which culminated in the creation of her germinal 1977 work *The White Goddess*.

Working with Contemporary Dancers was similarly meaningful for other emergent Canadian choreographers. It was a chance to flex creative muscle, to try out choreographic skill and to develop ideas in a stable company situation. Jennifer Mascall created her ominously titled *The Light at the End of the Tunnel May Be A Train*, Karen Jamieson made *Snakes and Ladders*, Paula Ravitz choreographed *Inside Out*, a group work, Judith Marcuse made *Re-Entry* and *Celebration*, set to music by Bach as played by harpsichordist Wanda Landowska. All these artists made their work for Contemporary Dancers during the 1970's, quite early in their choreographic careers. Having Rachel take a risk on their creative powers by inviting them to work with the company was a big vote of confidence.

Meanwhile, Rachel continued to invite choreographers from outside the country. Eminent American choreographer Cliff Keuter, noted for his dark narratives, whodunnits of dance, worked with the company. His *Plaisirs d'Amour* was performed in the fall season in 1975. Norman Morrice, British choreographer and director of Ballet Rambert, created *Fragments from a Distant Past* for the company's January, 1976 performances.

During the 1975-76 season Contemporary Dancers mounted David Earle's *Mirrors* in its October performances. Working with a score by J.S. Bach, Rachel created *Five Cameos*, which was danced by company members James Davis, Charles Flanders, Kenneth Lipitz, Nancy Paris, David Tucker and Rachel herself. The work premiered in January, 1976. In their March, 1976 spring season the company performed Earle's *Baroque Suite* and *Angelic Visitations*. The company also premiered Linda Rabin's *Domino* in March of 1976.

This was a season of changes in the twelve-member company. Dancer Kenneth Lipitz became the company's assistant artistic director. His wife Shelley Ziebel joined the company as a dancer, as did Zella Wolofsky, who directed the apprentice program as well.

During the 1976-77 season the company's October program included Norbert Vesak's *The Gift to be Simple*, a new duet made by Rachel for Kenneth Lipitz and herself which she titled *Interiors*, Rabin's *Domino*, and an effervescent work by U.S. choreographer Rodney Griffin called *Rialto*, which parodied dance styles of the 1930's.

By 1977 the company was mounting work by Toronto-based Anna Blewchamp, who set *Homage* and *Baggage* for Contemporary Dancers. *Baggage* was premiered by the company in January, 1977. They also danced Rachel's *The Woman I Am*, and Cliff Keuter's *Plaisirs d'Amour*. Celebrated soloist Ze'eva Cohen was a guest of the company. Her four-part work *Mothers of Israel* was featured on the company's winter program.

In 1977 Rachel organized the first choreographic workshops for company members. These "Footnotes" performances were given in the company's studios on February 3, 4 and 5. The workshops rose out of Rachel's desire to cultivate talent within the company. The protected climate of these situations fostered work by a number of artists whose skill has continued to develop. Tedd Robinson, Conrad Alexandrowicz, Stephanie Ballard, Ruth Cansfield and Gaile Petursson-Hiley all began their choreographic explorations in the company's studios at the Augustine Church.

Today, Ruth Cansfield Dancers is a funded company with its sights on international touring. Conrad Alexandrowicz has gone on to fame and notoriety with his own company Wild Excursions Performance. His choreography has been widely admired in Canada for its unique blend of movement and text. His dance-play *The Wines of Tuscany* has been produced in Vancouver and at Toronto's Tarragon Theatre. Tedd Robinson became artistic director of Contemporary Dancers in 1984. He is noted as a choreographer of sophisticated, tragicomic works of theatrical dance. Stephanie Ballard went on to create works for Contemporary Dancers, to win the Chalmers Award and the Clifford E. Lee Award, and to work with the Margie Gillis Dance Foundation as a choreographer and artistic director. "I grew up as a choreographer," says Ballard, "with Rachel giving me strong support and clear, honest feedback."

⁓   ⁓   ⁓

During the time when David Williams was the company's administrator, Contemporary Dancers toured quite extensively in the United States. The company's U.S. appearances included performances in the summer of 1977 at Jacob's Pillow in Lee, Massachusetts. This was a prestigious engagement for the company at an important festival. Over the course of four of five days, they gave several performances, dancing Anna Blewchamp's *Baggage*, Norbert Vesak's *The Gift to be Simple* and alternating Rachel's solo *Cameo* with her duet *Interiors*. As well, the company danced at New York City's Delacorte Festival in Central Park, where they performed *The Gift to be Simple,* and at the Wolf Trap Festival in Virginia.

American dance writer Don McDonagh singled out the company at Jacob's Pillow as seemingly most interested in dramatic dance, as opposed to the abstraction of pure dance. Writing for *The New York Times* on August 25, 1977, he said, "Rachel Browne...choreographed and danced *Interiors*, a melancholy duet for herself and Kenneth Lipitz that had its sunny moments but always carried an undertone of sadness. The performance was economical and Miss Browne's restrained dramatic intensity was very effective."

Fred Mathews, a Limón teacher noted for his refined musicality, was important in the company and school at this period. He made *Lunaris*, a work for the company, which premiered in October, 1977. On the same October program Rachel premiered her work *Just About Us*, a duet which she danced with company member Suzanne Oliver.

Occupied by the company for two or three years, the Princess Street studio was a fourth-floor space, a place of pillars and stairs. As an eleven-year-old student at Contemporary Dancers' school, Karen Kuzak was waiting in the lobby for her class time. Suddenly someone near her whispered, "That's Rachel Browne!" After this first sighting of Rachel, Kuzak remembers watching for her, an intense, small woman with long, dark hair, looking through the window at classes, keeping an eye on things. She remembers wanting to do well when Rachel was observing.

Gaile Petursson-Hiley studied ballet at the Royal Winnipeg Ballet. She also studied at other Winnipeg studios, restless, looking for an inspiration which she could not define. Almost by accident she went to Contemporary Dancers one day, when Fred Mathews was giving a class. The sweep of the movement, the musicality and kinetic excitement of the class enthralled her. "Oh my God," she remembers thinking, "this was happening in Winnipeg and I didn't know…"

Dancer Suzette Sherman had a similar experience. She came from a ballet background, but coming into contact with contemporary dance changed her mind. She auditioned for Rachel in New York, and went to Winnipeg as an apprentice. Sherman realized that she needed to pay attention to this way of dancing. Subsequently, she has enjoyed a long dancing career; for almost twenty years she was a principal member of the Toronto Dance Theatre, and remains choreographer David Earle's muse and partner in the dance.

In such ways, Rachel's work continued to touch young dancers' lives. She was a catalyst, a mentor, her influence far-reaching. At the same time, she was balancing her own creative needs with the larger scenario of her company. She was still dancing through the 1970's, her responsibilities and her ongoing love of dancing competing for her attention.

Tedd Robinson recalls not quite knowing what to make of Rachel's behaviour. On tour, if the company stopped for gas, Robinson remembers that it was Rachel's habit to leap out onto the pavement. Even in the dead of winter, she would jog around on the icy gravel a little, then hang onto the gas pump and do a few tendus and pliés. Anything to keep herself going.

When the company was travelling by air, Rachel had a habit of moving around from seat to seat on the plane. Sometimes she got lunch twice this way, which always surprised and delighted her. Dancers remember that Rachel, always needing to eat, travelled with bags of groceries. It was something of an initiation that the newest members of the company carried Rachel's bags for her. At receptions, Rachel, who hates waste, would sometimes go right back into the kitchen. The next day she would offer the company members reception leftovers for lunch.

Rachel led a complicated life, but was beginning to be acknowledged. In 1977 she was named "Woman of the Year" through the Winnipeg YWCA in recognition of her contributions to the enrichment of Winnipeg's cultural life.

For the company's January, 1978 performances Rachel programmed Anna Blewchamp's *Homage*, Judith Marcuse's *Re-Entry*, a remount of Paul Sanasardo's *Metallics* and Lynne Taylor-Corbett's *Spy in the House of Love*, a work based on Anaïs Nin's novel of the same name.

Rachel presented an extraordinary program in Contemporary Dancers' March, 1978 season. The company danced Anna Blewchamp's *Baggage*, Rachel's *Interiors* and the premiere of a beautiful work by Norman Morrice, *Songs*, set to Cantaloube's sumptuous *Songs of the Auvergne*. As well, renowned dance historian, dancer and choreographer Annabelle Gamson was a guest artist with the company. She performed a number of solos by Isadora Duncan, *Waltzes* (1913), *Mother* (1921) and *Étude* (1922), Mary Wigman's *Dance of Summer* (1929) and several of her own solo choreographies on these March programs.

In October of 1978 the company remounted work by David Earle, Cliff Keuter and Norbert Vesak, as well as Rachel's duet *Just About Us*. At the Playhouse Theatre in January, 1979, the company premiered a new group work by Rachel. Set to a score by Johannes Brahms, the work was titled *Solitude*. Lynne Taylor-Corbett's *Diary* also premiered at the Playhouse. The company restaged Taylor-Corbett's *Spy in the House of Love*, and Judith Marcuse's *Re-Entry*. Judith Lander, musician and composer, a dynamic presence onstage, performed Taylor-Corbett's work with the company.

Contemporary Dancers embarked on an extensive tour from February to April of 1979. Rachel programmed Sophie Maslow's *Country Music*, Taylor-Corbett's *Diary*, American choreographer Rodney Griffin's popular work *Rialto*, Vesak's ardent "Shaker" dance, *The Gift to be Simple*, and *Cameo*, a solo which she danced, set to music by J.S. Bach. The company performed right across the United States.

The Unquiet Bed

The woman I am
is not what you see
I'm not just bones
and crockery

the woman I am
knew love and hate
hating the chains
that parents make

longing that love
might set men free
yet hold them fast
in loyalty

the woman I am
is not what you see
move over love
make room for me

—Dorothy Livesay

During these years of diverse and intense activity, Rachel kept making dances, about one new work a year through the 1970's. Her choreography continued to evolve.

In 1975 Rachel choreographed *The Woman I Am*, using text by poets Dorothy Livesay and Miriam Mandel to accompany the group of dancers. The work was about forty minutes long, the longest dance she had made up to that time. Following a suggestion by Rosalie Goldstein, Rachel contacted musician Paul Horn, who created a score for the work. Horn, a flautist in Victoria, B.C., had shot to fame in hippie days with *Inside*, a haunting, otherworldly album which he recorded inside the Taj Mahal. Rachel's board of directors, sensing an opportunity to profit by the musician's celebrity, saw box office dollars in front of their eyes and pressed for a major national tour.

Rachel questioned the wisdom of taking the company on the road with such overt aspirations to hit the financial big time. Contemporary Dancers did undertake the tour with the Paul Horn Quintet, playing in the largest houses across the country. The tour was a success on some fronts, for it did show the company in new venues. As well, *The Woman I Am* was a strong work, made memorable through the use of the poetry and by Paul Horn's evocative score. Rachel comments that there was experimentation and creative growth visible in the dance. Financially, the tour was less of a success. Contemporary Dancers lost a good deal of money, by Rachel's estimate at least $40,000.

Toronto journalist Lawrence O'Toole gave the company a rave review, calling it "an exceptional troupe" during 1976 performances at the Art Gallery of Ontario. In *The Globe and Mail*, February 11, 1976, he wrote, "The company's look is found, I think, in *The Woman I Am*, in which the dancing—all clean and flowing lines—seems to come from some calm centre. You can see it in Browne's dancing with the company for a short bit...the choreography is mostly warmth—side bends where the arms form arcs and the palms of the hands are slightly cupped, leisurely extensions, slow formations of chains of dancers, and lifts where the dancer succumbs, supine, to her partner. The dancers have developed emotional relationships that shine through and extend the physical relationships the choreography has already built."

Rachel considers *Interiors* (1976), one of the duets she made for herself and Kenneth Lipitz, a "good" dance. Jim Donahue, a Winnipeg composer, wrote and performed a score for voice and guitar. Donahue sang words taken directly from work by Winnipeg-born poet Dorothy

Livesay, one of Rachel's favourite writers. *Interiors* was the story of a lost love.

In the *Village Voice* on September 26, 1977, New York critic Deborah Jowitt wrote of *Interiors*, "The dance, simple and meditative, deals with a woman (Browne) remembering a lost love (Kenneth Lipitz, who enters to dance with her). Browne is a quiet dancer, not virtuostic, a bit stiff, but I liked watching her. Some of the ideas bring to mind certain dance-dramas of the 1950's, in that movement often is chosen for its gestural appropriateness: Browne quivers a foot, a hand, lightly and stiffly against the air, as if she were creating the feeling, if not the literal shape, of brushing dust from a polished surface. The dance seems unnaturally prolonged and weighted, though, and the sweetly repetitive music emphasizes this."

Rachel says that *Interiors*, and a couple of other duets she performed with Ken Lipitz, were her best work of the mid-to-late 1970's. Lipitz was Rachel's assistant director for six seasons, from 1975-1980, and frequently her dance partner. Rachel speaks of him as a "wonderful, skilled dancer with a fluid ballet technique," talents she used in creating with him. *The Other* (1978), which had text by Dorothy Livesay and Adrienne Rich spoken live by the dancers, is a duet she also mentions as a "good" dance. *Just About Us* (1977), a duet Rachel created and performed with Suzanne Oliver, was another collaboration with Jim Donahue. This dance was about Rachel and her daughter Ruth. *Just About Us* was significant, in a long process of gradual change, as one of her first directly personal dances. Rachel says, "It was dedicated to my daughter Ruth and it was a mother-daughter relationship full of conflict and love and caring..." All of these were works of substance and intensity; they had nothing to do with pleasing audiences, or other dancers.

Rachel reflects, "In the company I kept saying, 'I am doing what I want to do.' I made two or three dances with Ken Lipitz, duets, in my middle period, which came right out of my guts. And that was about it, for my middle period."

If she felt unrealized as a choreographer, Rachel did not show it to her company. "I wouldn't have admitted it at the time," she says. Thinking back, she reflects, "Maybe my creative vistas were limited by my torn allegiances as a dancer and creator...Maybe I liked some of what I created, the 'serious stuff'—set to Bach, Mahler, Bartók, Ravel, Brahms, my solos, *Solitude*, for the company, the Mahler, *Where the Shining Trum pets Blow*—and the 'popular stuff'—to Oscar Peterson, Odetta, Billy Graham…"

Rachel's earliest dances seemed to acknowledge her respect for the ideals of her training, which had become the creative conventions of the time. Her first works operated by guidelines of structure and were most often created in relation to existing music. Though Rachel broke away from her devotion to ballet, her beginning dances seemed to stem from a way of thinking about dance as a formal art, somehow solitary, as if isolated from real time.

Perhaps this was related to dance she had admired during formative periods. Perhaps it stemmed from a sense of respect for dance as an art in its own right, with its own "laws" of composition. Perhaps Rachel was influenced by ideas integral to choreography at the time about what should be shown on the stage, what form it should take and how it should resolve.

Yet even in her first dances Rachel showed a fondness for strong voices of women in poetry and song. Odetta's songs had inspired one of her very earliest, most enduringly satisfying suites of dances. Through the 1970's her work increasingly drew inspiration from her favourite writers, Dorothy Livesay and Adrienne Rich. Her middle period works marked a deepening of her commitment to women's words. Always a voracious reader, she started reading Canadian poets and finding ways to incorporate text and poetry with her dances, alone, over tape, or at times spoken live. *The Woman I Am* was entirely based on Dorothy Livesay's poetry. A strong feminist message began to be a recurrent source and theme of Rachel's work.

"I am doing what I want to do," was Rachel's sustaining mantra through these middle years. Yet she felt bound, unable to expand creatively, given the demands on her energies. In a way, she could not help but be compromised artistically by the complex perspective of Contemporary Dancers' needs which was her constant companion. Choreography continued to be a parallel stream to her dancing and her work as the company's director. Fundamental change was to come later in her choreography.

Rachel's relationship with her growing daughters was difficult. They often felt that she could not "hear" them when they talked about their lives and activities, being so bound up with her own work and her artistic concerns. They were critical of their mother's personal relationships.

Rachel's relationship with Annette, her youngest, was somewhat different. Annette danced right through her childhood. During her early teenage years she was enrolled in the professional program at the Royal Winnipeg Ballet. She often attended classes taught by her mother and went to Contemporary Dancers' summer schools. Rachel recalls her as a "very, very good dancer". It was exciting for her, Annette recalls, to already know some of her mother's dances and then to work on them in repertory classes. The two went about their business with professionalism. At times they practised together. Usually, they could keep a mother–daughter dynamic out of their dancing. But Annette left home before she was sixteen, when their relationship became too volatile. Their close and loving rapport took some years to rebuild.

On Valentine's Day, 1978, Rachel and Ben Sokoloff had their first date. Ben Sokoloff, who taught English at the University of Manitoba, was a fan of the Royal Winnipeg Ballet and invited Rachel to accompany him to a demonstration at the ballet school. It must have been a good date. They started to keep company. Rachel recalls being eager to marry Ben. Their wedding took place on February 20, 1981. Rachel and Ben held their reception at Contemporary Dancers' studios.

(Ray Minkoff) Rachel Browne, 1941

(Ray Minkoff) Rachel Browne, 1939

Rachel Browne,
Royal Winnipeg Ballet
studio shot,
1958–59 season
Photo: Campbell and Chipman

The New Century Dancers, 1953,
New York City
From left: Crystal Field, Pearl
(Drescher) Cousin, Rachel
Browne, Harriet Gendel,
Brunhilda Ruiz, Irving Burton,
Mary-Ann (behind group)

Royal Winnipeg Ballet, "Bluebird Variation"
from *The Sleeping Beauty*, 1960–61 season,
Rachel Browne and Richard Rutherford

Opposite top: *Odetta's Songs and Dances*, choreography by Rachel Browne, 1964;
quartet section of dance titled "Green, Green Rocky Road"
From left: Marilyn Lewis, Cheryl Belkin, Barbara Barsky, Cherie Smith Photo: J. Coleman Fletcher

Opposite bottom: *Visions Fugitives*, choreography by Nenad Lhotka, 1965
From left: Jill Lhotka, Janice Narvey, Marilyn Lewis, Rachel Browne, Jennifer Ingram
Photo: J. Coleman Fletcher

Above: *Evening in the Suburbs*, choreography by Rachel Browne, 1966
From left: Jill Lhotka (standing), Barbara Coiner (sitting), Carolynn (Art) Tetrault (kneeling)
Photo: J. Coleman Fletcher

Opposite top: *Anerca*, choreography by Rachel Browne, 1967
Dancer: Rachel Browne, solo section of dance entitled "Old Song Now"
Photo: J. Coleman Fletcher

Opposite bottom: *The Urge*, choreography by Rachel Browne, 1967
From left: Jennifer Ingram, Charlene Gordon, Barbara Barsky
Photo: J. Coleman Fletcher

Above: *Where the Shining Trumpets Blow*, choreography by Rachel Browne, 1968
From left: Carolynn (Art) Tetrault, Rachel Browne, Charlene Gordon
Photo: Peter Kaczmarek

Variations, choreography by Rachel Browne, 1969
Dancer: Rachel Browne
Photo: J. Coleman Fletcher

True Believer, choreography by Robert Moulton, 1969
Dancers: Rachel Browne, Ron Holbrook Photo: J. Coleman Fletcher

Opposite top: *The Bus*, 1971
In the windows left to right: Elaine Loo, Michele Presley, Holly Anne Savage Standing: 1st and 2nd,
crew members; 3rd, David Tucker; 4th, Barbara Johnson; 5th, Janet Oxley; 6th, Jim Green
On roof: left, David Weller; right, Charlie Moulton On hood: left, Larry Brinker; right, Rachel Browne

Opposite bottom: *Country Music*, choreography by Sophie Maslow, 1972
From left: Leslie Dillingham, Nancy Paris, Larry Brinker, Stephanie Ballard Photo: J. Coleman Fletcher

Above: *The Woman I Am*, choreography by Rachel Browne, 1975
Dancer: Stephanie Ballard Photo: Jim Stadnick

Cameo, choreography by Rachel Browne, 1975
Dancer: Rachel Browne
Photo: Andrew Oxenham

The Gift to be Simple, choreography by Norbert Vesak, 1976
Dancer: Ken Lipitz

Above: *Spy in the House of Love*, **choreography by Lynn Taylor Corbett, 1976**
Dancers: Rachel Browne (standing), Nancy Paris, James Davis (floor) Photo: David Hiley

Opposite top: *Interiors*, choreography by Rachel Browne, 1976
Dancers: Rachel Browne, Ken Lipitz Photo: Gerry Kopelow

Opposite bottom: *Baggage*, choreography by Anna Blewchamp, 1977
Dancers: Sara Brummel, Grant McDaniel Photo: Andrew Oxenham

Above: *The Murder of George Keuter*, choreography by Cliff Keuter, 1978
Dancers from front: Grant McDaniel, Seth Walsh, Ken Lipitz, Kim Hughes

Opposite: *The Other*, choreography by Rachel Browne, 1978
Dancers: Rachel Browne, Ken Lipitz
Photo: Robert Tinker

Above: *Celebration*, choreography by Judith Marcuse, 1979
Dancer: Gaile Petursson-Hiley photo: David Cooper

Opposite top: *Anna*, choreography by Stephanie Ballard, presented by Stephanie Ballard and
Dancers, 1987 From left: Ruth Cansfield, Odette Heyn-Penner, Gaile Petursson-Hiley, Faye
Thomson, Anne Bruce Falconer Photo: Jim Kacki

Opposite bottom: *My Romance*, choreography by Rachel Browne, 1990
Dancer: Sharon Moore Photo: Bruce Monk

Above: *Pat's Bach*, choreography by Rachel Browne, 1991
Dancer: Patricia Fraser Photo: Cylla von Tiedemann

Opposite top: *Mouvement*, choreography by Rachel Browne, 1992
Dancer: Alana Shewchuk
Photo: Bruce Monk

Opposite bottom: *K.J.4*, choreography by Rachel Browne,
mounted for Professional Program of Contemporary Dancers in 1994
From left: Linnea Swan, Liz Cooper, Erin Flynn, Sherri Rice
Photo: Matthew Parker

Above: *Toward Light*, choreography by Rachel Browne, 1995
Dancer: Sharon Moore
Photo: Bruce Monk

Opposite: Rachel Browne, studio shot, 1996
Photo: Gerry Kopelow

Edgelit, choreography by Rachel Browne, 1997
Dancer: Davida Monk
Photo: Gavin Semple

A COUP

Odette Heyn-Penner remembers Rachel performing the lead role in Lynne Taylor Corbett's work *Spy in the House of Love*. Heyn-Penner recalls her standing in front of a rocking chair which was the set for the work; a woman of experience and maturity, an authoritative presence on the stage. Though other dancers took on that role, though Rachel was actually second cast and company dancer Shelley Ziebel first, Heyn-Penner's recollection is that no one else could approach the knowledge and clarity with which Rachel danced the part. This image of Rachel dancing remained vivid twenty years after the performance.

Gaile Petursson-Hiley later danced the same role. She also recalls watching Rachel's artistry and experience. Rehearsal with Rachel was an illuminating process, recalls Petursson-Hiley. Rachel was keen to help the younger dancer understand the detailed nuance with which she approached every moment of the work—the musicality, the physicality, the dramatic import of each phrase and gesture. Petursson-Hiley remembers that Taylor-Corbett and composer Judith Lander wanted Rachel to dye her greying hair. Rachel declined, though while the creators were still around she appeased them by putting some shoe polish in her hair. Others recall that her wild, silvering hair was striking in performance.

Rachel's daughters recall her serene face and the intensity of her focus. The stage continued to be a place of refuge, a place of no compromise, a place where there could be no other demands. Onstage Rachel was expert and charismatic. Into her forties, she was still dying to dance. Being on the stage, being only in the present moment, was a sustaining happiness. Rachel's power was in her dancing, in the practice of her art. Her magic circle, the stage, remained a place of calm and authority for her. Karen Kuzak recalls watching Rachel in the early

1980's dancing *Haiku*, a duet she created for Ruth Cansfield and herself in 1981. Kuzak's memory is of "how strikingly beautiful" Rachel was, her beauty "having to do with her face and her heart".

Annette remembers her mother as an elegant, serious dancer. "I could totally relate," she says. As a teenager, she did not always make distinctions about what work she saw her mother dancing, whether it was a solo by one of the company's guest choreographers, or a work she had made herself. For Annette, the pride was all in the force of her mother's stage presence, whether she was performing traditional or more innovative work. Annette and her mother could talk about dance for hours. Not so much about what choreography meant, but about the dancing itself.

In 1979 Contemporary Dancers hired administrator Tom Scurfield, who came from a background in theatre and the insurance business. He was an active and quite successful manager for the company, but as a team, he and Rachel were ill-suited. Rachel discusses issues as though she is inspecting diamonds, turning them over, examining every facet in the light. Scurfield had a more bluff style and a commanding male energy—like oil and water with Rachel's approach. Still, says Rachel, they might have found a way to work together.

Scurfield had a heated exchange with the board in which he insisted on acquiring full executive powers—the power to hire and fire any member of the company, including Rachel. Although he assured Rachel that he had no intention of using this power to oust her, Rachel was put on her guard.

At the time the board chairman was a businessman named Rick Muller. He wanted to run the company in a very strong manner, including involvement with the company's artistic planning. Rachel resisted this, feeling that the board members' role was to assist with the financial health and stability of the organization, with no artistic input. Once again, Rachel faced attempts by management and her board to assume power within the company. After unsuccessful attempts to rebalance Scurfield's management needs with Rachel's artistic needs, the board let Scurfield go. Later, it became clear that the company was in a state of some financial distress.

When Scurfield moved on, the board hired Evelyn Polish. She came to the company from a background in management and community work. Rachel recalls her, at the time of her hiring, as an attractive, dynamic woman. Contemporary Dancers was a first venture for her into the life of a professional performing arts organization. Evelyn Polish was to stay with the company for ten years.

By this point Rachel had been at the helm of Contemporary Dancers for nearly nineteen years. Her family was almost grown. It was Rachel's fond hope that Annette would follow in her footsteps. By the time Annette was fifteen, mother and daughter took class together when they travelled to New York. Annette recalls this as an amazing experience. To be in the same class as her mother gave her a feeling of great joy and satisfaction. They were there for different reasons, Annette to dance and work on her technique, Rachel to dance and to seek stimulation from fresh ideas about teaching class, musicality, alignment and physicality. Rachel, though she felt she was nearly past her prime as a dancer, recalls Annette earnestly saying to her after classes, "You were the best one."

Changing ideas were circulating in the dance world. The Canada Council had identified creation as the soul of contemporary dance. Companies founded to promote and produce the work of single choreographers were on the rise, as many young dance artists sought the means to pursue their individual artistic visions. Points were going to young creators for the innovative ways in which they conceived and staged their work. Attention was increasingly on the Montreal dance scene. Contemporary dance, phoenix-like by tradition, was being remade, this time around by the influence of the radical revisioning of New York's post-modern pedestrianism, the anything-goes inclusiveness of contact dance and the extravagant risk-taking of Montreal danse théâtre. The rise of musical minimalism, with its alternative sense of harmony and structural development, also influenced the dance world.

Rachel's vision for her repertory company had very different roots.

Despite her inclusion of new young choreographers in the company's programs, Contemporary Dancers was looking very different from what was "hot" by the late 1970's and early 1980's. Robert Desrosiers was making his dreamscapes. Danny Grossman was finding success with his first choreography. Jean-Pierre Perreault was edging toward his landmark work *Joe*. International acclaim was imminent for Edouard Lock and Ginette Laurin. Rachel continued to make her serious works, and her lighter ones. She continued to make efforts to deepen and change her vision.

In 1980 Rachel attended a month-long National Choreographic Seminar at the Banff Centre. The seminar was directed by Robert Cohan, choreographer and artistic director of the London Contemporary Dance Theatre, and Todd Bolender, whose work she had performed in her New York City years with the Ryder-Frankel company. She worked to address the creative challenges of this pressure-cooker situation, which set choreographers a new creative challenge each day, allowing limited rehearsal time in which to work out their ideas, with daily discussion of the results. She was determined to renew her choreographic vision and to extend the range of her skills.

When Stephanie Ballard became associate artistic director of Contemporary Dancers, the company began to transform from within.

In the overall climate of change, Ballard's choreographic ambitions were fired by her early success in creating for the company. In 1979, in the first Dance Discovery, a shared project of Contemporary Dancers and Royal Winnipeg Ballet, she showed *Sympathetic Magic* and *Mahler Duet*. She premiered *Prairie Song* in the May, 1980, Dance Discovery series. *Prairie Song* and *A Christmas Carol*, and other early works she created for the company, brought her critical attention. In 1980 she premiered *The Snow Goose*, a work for young audiences.

As Rachel recalls, within a year or two of the expansion of Stephanie's responsibilities in the company, Ballard and Evelyn Polish found that they shared many ideas about the company's potential and future directions. A number of the dancers in the company loved working with Ballard. There was some discontent among the dancers over Rachel's artistic choices and her direction of the company. Dancers' loyalties began to realign. Feelings of frustration and discontent started to ferment. Gaile Petursson-Hiley recalls criss-crossing the United States on a demanding seven-week tour in this unsettled atmosphere. At close quarters with the company members, many of them ready to leave, Rachel must have had a strained time of it. By 1981 the turmoil within the company was overt, but Rachel carried on.

Although she recalls these months as a very uneasy time, Rachel did not suspect the precariousness of her directorship. Professional dancers often have strong but fragile egos. Dancers need to be challenged artistically, to be coached dramatically, to have classes which equip them to meet the physical demands of the dances they perform. Dancers often find it difficult to see past these immediate needs and often are not really encouraged to do so. Directors, dancers and choreographers get used to heavy weather and to working in thorny circumstances. The work progresses despite difficulties. It is often this way. Rachel, by her own admission never terribly astute politically, was consumed with the needs of creation and the pressing claims of the company's daily life.

But there were warnings. There were meetings among the dancers. It was suggested that they should speak out about the reasons for their discontent. Gaile Petursson-Hiley recalls going with Tedd Robinson to talk to Rachel. The two dancers wanted to let Rachel know that many company members were not satisfied with the kind of direction Rachel was giving them. They wanted to inform her of the spreading sense that the company was not being strongly led. Perhaps Rachel was naive. Her tenacity had been a sustaining strength and also, at times, had clouded her vision.

Despite the rumblings within the company, Rachel continued to make work with the dancers. One piece she mentions is *M.L.W.*, named for celebrated American jazz pianist Mary Lou Williams. This dance, says Rachel, was made in 1981, with the experience of the Banff Choreographic Seminar not far behind her. She was attempting to discard some of her old approaches to choreography and try something new. Without preparing steps before she went into rehearsal, she worked with D-Anne Kuby, Ruth Cansfield, Gaile Petursson-Hiley and Karen Unsworth, creating movement material through directed improvisation. Part of the dance was a strong, aggressive trio, which echoed some of the feelings roiling through the company. Rachel made an intense solo for D-Anne Kuby to a jazz version of *Somewhere Over the Rainbow* —no irony intended. Some of the dance, Rachel reflects, worked, but it was an uphill battle; her creative energies were focused on survival.

In retrospect, Rachel has said, she can see that her meetings with

Stephanie Ballard and Evelyn Polish became an indication of the direction in which things were going. Rachel recalls strange tensions when the three women discussed the company. Polish grew angry with her very easily. Ballard, acutely conflicted by her high regard for Rachel, her belief in her own talent and her own needs for the future, was decidedly uncomfortable. At one board meeting Polish spoke out about Rachel in her presence.

"She...let the cat out of the bag, speaking very harshly about me...saying something to the effect of, 'Well, the whole point of Stephanie's frustration is that here she is, capable and young and able to do all these things and here you are entrenched and holding her back and not allowing her to take over such and such responsibility and then keeping her down, so of course she's angry, of course she's frustrated...'."

The board of directors had formed a production committee. Rachel recalls that it came to insist that its suggestions be taken. The board commissioned a work called *Now I'm John* from Lynne Taylor-Corbett. Their aim was to have a work for the company repertory, with music by John Lennon, to be performed near the anniversary of Lennon's death. Rachel was opposed to this initiative, as the idea did not come from the creator. The board, forcefully led by Rick Muller, continuing as chairman, proposed that the company present *Now I'm John* in performances at the National Arts Centre in Ottawa. Rachel felt that it was not Taylor-Corbett's best work and not compelling enough artistically to show at the National Arts Centre, an important venue for dance nationally. A critical, sophisticated audience would be in attendance, as would Canada Council staff.

Rachel did not agree with arguments that the dance would attract large audiences. But the board's pressure, Rachel recalls, caused both her and Ballard, her associate director, to feel obligated to present *Now I'm John*. They capitulated. The company was not well-received at the National Arts Centre.

During this period Rachel asked to see Canada Council assessments of the company. Although the assessors' names were confidential and the Council's policy at that time was to release only parts of assessors' comments to artists, the tone of the assessments was surprising to Rachel—surprisingly positive. She felt that in the larger dance community there was still faith in her ability to direct and make good artistic choices for her company.

The jist of comments from assessors, from 1980 through 1982, was that the company was attractive, competent and professional. Contemporary Dancers was lauded for the diversity of its programming although, despite flashes of inspiration, the work was seen to be lacking in excitement and innovation. Rachel was praised as a director for building the company's repertory and developing company choreographers. She was also noted for her performing abilities and her mature artistry, particularly in performances of Doris Humphrey's historically important work *Two Ecstatic Themes*.

Stephanie Ballard has said of Rachel, "She always openly talked about and instilled in me a strong sense of it being okay to agree to disagree." This principle perhaps also made Rachel feel that it was alright to press on with the company, that things would work out. From Rachel's point of view it was a difficult time, but she and Ballard were managing to live with disagreement and still getting on with their work. For Ballard, it was a wrenching, divisive time.

The company continued to be plagued by financial problems carried over from earlier administration. Because of this, a sense of liability and dissatisfaction at the board level brewed with management's agitation and ongoing artistic unrest. Rick Muller considered Evelyn Polish a superb manager. It is Rachel's perception that, in light of this, he endorsed Polish's belief in Stephanie Ballard as a new leader for the company.

By the closing months of 1982, the situation had deteriorated to a point of no return. Some of the board members had said they would stand by Rachel, but the balance tipped. Rachel was the victim a coup engineered from within the company. She was ousted by the board, and called down by the dancers.

"The whole board was won over to the side of Rick Muller and Evelyn Polish, who were convinced that all they had to do was get rid of me and the money would come flowing in from the Canada Council..." said Rachel.

Moti Shojani, an ally of Rachel's on the board of directors, came to speak to her one evening. Rachel was rehearsing at Contemporary Dancers' studios. She was always there, day and night; Shojani had no difficulty finding her. She had come to tell Rachel of the board's decision to ask her to step down as artistic director.

"It was as if somebody had punched me out, or I had gotten run over by an automobile, or somebody had taken me and hit me forcefully against the wall…I just could not believe it, I was aghast, I was speechless, I was weeping."

Despite Rachel's disbelief, Moti Shojani's message was true. The board had decided to fire her.

Rachel remembers telephoning Ben. They had been having a disagreement of some kind, which was put aside entirely. He came and picked her up.

⁊   ⁊   ⁊

Rachel is thoughtful about this traumatic turning point, and philosophical about the choices she made. Her continuing presence in Contemporary Dancers has affected the company's development. At the time of the coup, she insisted on remaining relevant to this entity which she had birthed. As well, she instinctively protected her own needs through ensuring that she would have opportunities to teach and create and dance, all important to her survival as an artist.

While these changes were going on, they were very painful. Besides the loss of the direction of the company she had founded, another deep wound for Rachel was the sense of being "outgrown" by people she had nurtured.

All of this occurred just before the company's Christmas break in 1982. Rachel was handed a letter by D-Anne Kuby the morning of the day she left for vacation. She recalls seeing Gaile Petursson-Hiley and Ruth Cansfield working on something on the typewriter in the company's office. Later she realized that it was this document.

Rachel did not open the letter until she was on the airplane. She knew that it would not be an easy letter to read. She had heard reports of the dancers' grumbling from the board, but the dancers themselves had not spoken of the scope of their discontent directly to her. Sitting with her elderly mother, with Annette and Annette's boyfriend on the airplane, Rachel started to read. She was profoundly shocked.

"I don't think that time will ever be duplicated in terms of the trauma I felt. This was a whole long, long listing of negative statements about me and my way of rehearsing dancers, my choreography, my way of teaching, the way I give notes, my organizational abilities, the way I make up the schedule, the way I deal with the dancers. Many of them I brought right through the ranks, right from novices, because I believed in their talent. And all of them had signed, the whole company had signed this letter... I knew that these were my last days."

It isn't hard to picture—Rachel, already isolated by her leadership role, desolate, feeling entirely betrayed. But although she was devastated emotionally, her inner strength came to her rescue.

At the time Rachel was reading a book by Dr. Albert Ellis, a proponent of rational emotive therapy. She remembers hanging onto this book as if it were a bible, something real for her to cling to. She felt that if she could remember all the positive things about herself, she could live through this. She knew that much of what she was reading from the dancers' point of view was a contrived list—Rachel has always been quite unpretentious about her talent and skill. She knew that although she was not perfect, in many ways she was a very good director. The loss of the company was a source of great sorrow to her, but it would not depress her to the point where she could not function.

Rachel's Miriam was twenty when her mother was ousted from Contemporary Dancers. Looking back, she finds her mother's steadfastness nothing short of amazing. At the time, she found it rather difficult to assess the blow that had been struck her mother. But she remembers watching Rachel fight her way back to repute and position.

From the ashes of the attack on her work and her world, Rachel took a radical position. She began to look at her situation in a wider way. She asked herself what would be the worst possible scenario. If she were unable to teach or choreograph, if she could not perform, if she could not take class and continue to maintain herself physically as a dancer, if these things were taken away from her, she wondered what she would do with her life.

In the contemplation of the awful emptiness that these losses would bring into her life, Rachel found that there would be ways for her to bring her beliefs to bear.

"If my love of dance were ripped away from me, I could still do something worthwhile and meaningful and good with my life…I would have my family, whom I adore. I could devote myself to peace and to helping other people and to working against pollution of the environment."

These thoughts comforted Rachel and gave her courage to go on. It is a measure of her generosity, and the deep moral questioning that has guided her, that she has been able to assist some of the people who helped to bring her down as artistic director of Contemporary Dancers. Some of them have faced similar situations of being jockeyed out of position.

A number of years later, Gaile Petursson-Hiley was suddenly faced with censure in a meeting with dancers in the Dance Collective which she started with Ruth Cansfield. Petursson-Hiley asked for a few minutes of solitude in which to collect her thoughts. She sat for a few moments, then telephoned Rachel. Rachel, she recalls, counselled her calmly, helping to make certain options clear, with no hint of interference.

On consideration, Rachel has realized that the members of Contemporary Dancers were in a sense "pawns", that the board and management may have fanned their ambient dissatisfactions to fuel its own intentions. Dance companies are like fields of grass. Negativity travels like wildfire. The slightest breeze of discontent can send the whole thing up in flames in an instant. Rachel was on the receiving end of this cruel truth, but she was able to see it eventually for what it was. Dancers who were in the company at the time remorsefully echo the sense of having been caught up in something that they did not fully understand.

Since 1983 Rachel has observed similar power struggles in other dance organizations. At the time of her dismissal from the company, though, she did not know that such issues were not unusual. There was a time factor too. The founders of Canadian companies began to be challenged by younger artists during the 1980's, when available funds began to level out and soon were fully committed to established companies. Younger artists raised their opinions about the "haves" and the "have-nots" of Canadian dance, targeting established companies as places where historical inequity needed to be redressed. Younger artists needed money to do their work too.

At the time, Rachel had only her own experience to look to. She considered that the roots of the company's problems must be in her own inadequacy. In the years since then, from watching the work of succeeding directors, seeing that they have faltered on occasion, she has also been able to verify her belief that she did her job very well.

Meanwhile, Rachel's work was woven through the core of the company. It was her life's work. She was not an itinerant choreographer and teacher. She did not have other jobs lined up. She had not been interested in travelling around the country to teach and make dances by commission. Contemporary Dancers was her dance house, the situation she had built for two decades as her place to dance, her ground for creation.

Losing the company was, in a sense, the end of Rachel's world. She had not even thought of a life after Contemporary Dancers.

So when the possiblity of keeping her association with the company came up, she became wily. She decided that if she was going down, then she did not want to give away this plum, as she felt the company to be.

Rachel decided to fight. She joined forces with a couple of board members who remained her allies. She stipulated to the board that she would step down, but that there would be a formal search process for a new artistic director. After resigning, Rachel was appointed interim artistic director of the company. She agreed to assist the board in seeking a new artistic director.

The company's search broadened beyond Canada. Bill Evans, a Seattle-based modern dance teacher and choreographer, was hired. Rachel says that it was her hope that she could reach an understanding with him and maintain an association with the company, teaching and perhaps becoming one of the company's resident choreographers. She wanted to hang onto some part of the company, even in a compromised way.

Rachel speculates that if she had left at the time of the coup, she might have been less wounded when she was finally shut out of the company entirely. Some people close to her accused her of acting desperately, trying to hold onto anything at all. In another way, she reflects, it was wise of her to return to Contemporary Dancers, because maintaining some access to certain company resources did satisfy some of her intrinsic needs.

At the same time, Rachel feels she was used by the board. As she looks back, she thinks she played into the hands of board members, who were manipulating her actions. They no longer had to deal with her as the company's artistic director, as they felt she was a detriment to the company. But at the same time they were getting the benefit of her intensive knowledge of the dance field to help them search for a new artistic director and keep the company operating.

Rachel's fortitude and her love of dance sustained her.

Even through her despair, she worked. In the winter months of 1983 she had no heart for creating with the company's dancers, who had spoken out so vehemently against her. The dancers had no desire to work with her.

She worked alone. She worked surreptitiously in the church's Guild Hall, a room which was not supposed to be used by the company. But it was quiet and empty during the day. In the dim light, Rachel moved the tables and chairs, clearing out the big space. She listened to Bach and did what she always did. Rachel danced. *Shalom*, the work she made then, she considers one of her strongest solo dances. She recalls that the ambiance of this twilight place was very much part of the dance.

Shalom was the only work of Rachel's to be shown in Contemporary Dancers' performances at Toronto's Premiere Dance Theatre that winter. The same was true of the company's spring performances in Winnipeg. The music she chose for the dance had been recorded by Glenn Gould. She was asked by Winnipeg journalist Jacqui Good if the work was a tribute to Gould, who had recently died. Perhaps it was.

Shalom was also an elegy for her very private grief at the loss of her company. Making the dance and performing it, Rachel says, saved her sanity. She knew, through it, that even though she had lost the company, she was not going to lose dance.

Alana Shewchuk, who has known Rachel since her childhood, remembers her in *Shalom*. Shewchuk speaks of how she and other members of Contemporary Dancers used to rifle through the "archives", a box of photographs kept in the basement at the company's studios. In this box is a photograph of Rachel as a young ballerina; serene, a spirit of dance musing. Shewchuk sustains a strong image of Rachel dancing *Shalom* with this same look of clarity and transcendence about her. A dancer at one with her dance.

There are many cases of acrimonious changes of artistic direction in arts organizations. In most cases, the damage remains unhealed. The pattern is traceable.

A gifted performing artist creates a context for her art. While she is challenged by instigating and guiding an organic entity through its wobbly, difficult first years, the artist's core intentions do not alter very much. She wants to practice her art.

If successful, the artist develops a board of directors and finds administration to support her artistic activity. She is quite quickly expected to speak the language of business, to develop a canny sense of politics, self-preservation and competitiveness. As the artistic entity grows and changes, so does the field around it. The artist, whose fresh energy was the reason for the company's original success, begins to look expendable. It looks, to board and administration, like good business to appoint someone new to the artistic helm.

Changes have come about in a number of dance companies in Canada. Because the art is young in this country, many of these directoral changes are happening for the first time. Because of the closely personal nature of the bond of artist and company common to modern dance, changes are often radical and excruciatingly painful. All the more remarkable, then, that Rachel negotiated her way through years of murky waters to a place of mutual understanding with Contemporary Dancers.

There are lessons to be gleaned from the survivors of such experiences. It is a kind of trial. The fact that Rachel would not give up or go away has distinguished Contemporary Dancers, not just among dance companies, but among all artistic enterprises. There is a way to honour beginnings and to value what has come before. By being there, Rachel has insisted that the honourable way be found.

In the end, what matters is that the artist emerges from turbulent times able to find a way to do what she needs to do. For Rachel, the shock of leaving Contemporary Dancers was a body blow, a rude shove into the necessity of finding a new configuration for her work and her life.

NEW BEGINNINGS

Bill Evans' tenure with the company lasted only one season, but during his time with Contemporary Dancers Rachel did continue to teach for the company and in the school. She created a new work, *A Jest of God*, inspired by Margaret Laurence's novel of the same name. As well, she became the company's development officer, soon proving herself valuable as a fundraiser. So, despite the wounds she had sustained, she was able to maintain her association with the company she loved.

When Bill Evans left, Tedd Robinson became the new artistic director. Rachel had brought Robinson to Winnipeg as an apprentice member of Contemporary Dancers. In time he had joined the company as a dancer. He describes how, after his first season with Contemporary Dancers, he wanted to go to Vancouver to work with Karen Jamieson, Terry Hunter and Savannah Walling in their company Terminal City. But he had already signed his contract for the coming season with Contemporary Dancers and Rachel held him to it.

It is always difficult to replace male dancers and Robinson, a unique presence onstage, had already had several roles created exclusively for him. It would have been daunting, if not impossible, to replace him at short notice and cost the company money and rehearsal time. So his signed contract was considered binding. Despite initial frustration, he recognized that Rachel always acted for the company's interests first. As it turned out, it was in his long-term interests to stay. Tedd Robinson became the resident choreographer, and, at the beginning of the 1984-85 season, artistic director. Contemporary Dancers was the place in which his choreographic and directorial careers blossomed.

Rachel knew Robinson to be a very mild person. Again, she turned this new situation into an advantage. She continued to teach for the school and company. Although she knew that Robinson was chiefly interested in pursuing his own work, she made arrangements with him to continue to choreograph. In so doing, she was ensuring herself an extended period of relative quiet during the years of his tenure as artistic director. During this time the company was called "Contemporary Dancers Canada".

Working from an original idea of Bill Evans', Robinson took over the Festival of Canadian Modern Dance. From an initial occurrence as an add-on to the company's 20th anniversary celebrations, the festival developed into an important national event which lasted from 1985 until 1992. Rachel's choreography was shown annually at these festivals.

Although her work was not of highest priority to Contemporary Dancers any longer, Rachel still felt satisfaction in being able to create. Her work and her teaching ensured her continuing influence in the company.

In March, 1985, the company staged performances called "Best of the Rep, 20th Anniversary Celebration". The program quoted guest choreographer Cliff Keuter saying, "This Company is exceptional. My work is done with understanding, commitment and more important, passion." Writing for *Dance in Canada* magazine, journalist Robert Enright called Contemporary Dancers "a dedicated, versatile and political company whose repertoire is less about movement than about the obsessions and celebration of the human spirit."

Rachel presented *To the New Year* in these performances, her latest in a series of politically-themed works. Writing for *Border Crossings* in the fall of 1985, arts journalist Jacqui Good commented that it was a successful marriage of a "small personal statement with a larger more universal message. To the New Year, a personal and powerful message piece, presents Rachel Browne as earth-mother, life source and evangelist all wrapped up in one." Good noted that the piece's use of original music by Winnipeg composer Diana McIntosh, along with poetry, visuals and dance, moved Rachel's work toward a new theatricality.

Responding to this observation, Rachel commented that she explores themes over a long time in her work. In this case, she said, the theatricality was a kind of culmination. "I think that some of the works along my particular thought stream have been *Haiku, The Other, To the*

Year 2000, Survival, A Jest of God and now the new one."

During Tedd Robinson's five years as director Rachel continued to make dances and consolidated her strength as a successful fundraiser for the company, earning new respect with the administration and the board. She had an office right outside the studio and was able to make a small salary from her work for Contemporary Dancers.

As time went by, the company was increasingly committed to the creation and performance of Robinson's work. A gifted creator, he moved ahead with the full support of the board. He was particularly encouraged by Ron Keenberg, heading the board, who believed fully in his talent. Robinson began to receive national acclaim for his wildly theatrical, highly entertaining work. Audiences found it both accessible and audacious. As Robinson's reputation and skill built, opportunities for other choreographers, Rachel included, began to decline.

These were years of success for the company. With great perseverance, Rachel enlisted major corporate sponsorship, which made financing the festivals possible. The month of May was declared "Modern Dance Month" in Winnipeg. The creative climate at Contemporary Dancers was very positive during Robinson's tenure. Perhaps, in some way, Rachel's own creativity was buoyed by this new climate of artistic risk and achievement. The years of stability at Contemporary Dancers helped restore her creative confidence. She began to see other possibilities for her own work.

As occasions for choreographing for Contemporary Dancers grew fewer, it began to seem to Rachel that the only way she might show her work would be to undertake some independent work, separate from the company. It occurred to her that she might seek support for independent projects from the Manitoba Arts Council. She says, "I don't know what bug got into my head…"

Gathering her nerve, she approached the Council and began to work with a few carefully chosen dancers.

⁓   ⁓   ⁓

Rachel dates leaving the company's directorship as the beginning of the change in her creative life. From an initial performance of her work, given in 1987, she has gradually expanded to her present status as a very active independent choreographer.

"Being kicked out of the directorship of Contemporary Dancers…allowed me to focus on what I love the most and what I find the hardest, to try to make dances. The only thing I was focusing on artistically was making dances… I still like to get up on a stage and perform, but in terms of a focus, it was really choreography. My needs as a performer didn't interest me that much. The big gap that I felt with my life…this finally trying to choreograph. Always feeling that I was not naturally gifted at it, that I had to work extremely hard at it to make it work. I just wanted to do it."

Painful experiences had compelled change, pushing her forward.

Over time, Rachel has resolved many conflicts with people. Choreographers Ruth Cansfield and Gaile Petursson-Hiley say she has been "two hundred percent supportive" in their creative careers. Rachel and Stephanie Ballard have resolved many issues. They are collegial artistic friends now. Both remain committed to the work of dance.

Ballard considers Rachel her mother in the dance. From her perspective, the split between them was part of the growth of her own individuality. She says of Rachel, "It's amazing that she came back again and again…Losing the company was painful, but put her in a really good place and allowed her the luxury of being rid of all that responsibility. She could start really taking choreography seriously—studying, observing, working."

She did.

Once she mobilized her energies, Rachel was a force. From 1987 to 1993 she presented six evening-length programs of her choreography in Winnipeg. Five of these were supported in part by the Manitoba Arts Council, which has been the most consistent source of support for her Winnipeg performances, and one by the Canada Council. She presented these programs, largely of new or recently created work, in 1987, 1989, 1990, 1991, 1992 and 1993.

In the first full evening of dance in Winnipeg, there were six works on the program, including *Haiku*, danced by Rachel and Ruth Cansfield, and *Old Times Now*, performed by D-Anne Kuby. Rachel used the Gas Station Theatre, across the street from Contemporary Dancers' studios in the Augustine Church.

"I gave my first performance of my own work—which I started to work on in 1986—I presented it in 1987. The first evening all of my own work, after so many years of creating. Even though some of the dances didn't work, there were some that I learned from, some substantial stuff. The next evening I prepared was in 1989 and again, there was maybe one work that really interested me, where I thought, 'Ah, there's some possibility for development.' And then I continued. I felt compelled to continue to create."

Journalist Jacqui Good spoke about Rachel's work on the CBC on June 20, 1987. She commented, "In the past, the individual dances I have seen have impressed me as being well-made and honest, but seeing all six together there was this great ringlet of power, very emotional. And I think I understand now much more the elements that make the Rachel Browne style distinctive…I think she harkens back to a time when modern dance saw itself as an answer to the overblown success of ballet, when emotion and movement were more important than all the trappings."

In June of 1989, Rachel presented a series of performances she called "Rachel Browne, A Retrospective". The performances were both a recounting of earlier works and a celebration of Contemporary Dancers' 25th anniversary. The program included an excerpt of *Odetta's Songs and Dances* (1964), an excerpt of *Solitude* (1975), *Old Times Now* (1987), *In a Dark Time the Eye Begins to See* (1987), *Sunset Sentences* and *Tres Bailes Enigmaticos*, commissioned by Winnipeg's Women and the Arts Festival in 1988.

Winnipeg journalist Robert Enright spoke about her work on the CBC on June 9, 1989. "It was a real celebration," he commented. "The dance community turned out in spades for it and the applause at the end of the performance was very warm indeed. They were basically paying tribute to a woman who in every sense of the term has been a pioneer in modern dance in this city, and, I dare say, in the country as well."

Enright spoke about the development of Rachel's work, noting the loveliness of her early dances *Odetta's Songs and Dances* and *Solitude*.

Even then, Enright said, the viewer could see "right below the surface of her dances, a strong commitment to women's issues and to using dance as a vehicle for changing society in a political way." With later work, such as *In a Dark Time the Eye Begins to See*, he noted the "intensification of the feeling of being a woman in a man's world, or at least a world that was going to do damage to everyone." *Old Times Now*, which was danced by AnneBruce Falconer, concluded the program. "It brought the house down," said Enright, "and was a very bluesy, gusty, sexy and powerful way of ending the evening."

Enright went on to speak of Rachel's achievements with Contemporary Dancers. "The company," he said, "went through some extremely hard times financially and emotionally and she stuck with it all the way, with a kind of dignity and courage that have always characterized her own life and her belief that dance is a vehicle, actually, for social change."

By 1994 Rachel was able to reflect, "It does feel like a new beginning. It started when I was pushed out of the company. I don't feel as inadequate as a choreographer. I got a small grant to preserve some of my very old dances. Looking at some of those dances, I thought, 'Oh, I really could make dances, so maybe I'm not so inadequate as I thought...' I wasn't judging the seasoned choreographer, I was just looking at the raw talent. It gave me encouragement. Wonderful to feel myself coming full circle. I learned a lot from looking at those dances and seeing from where I had come."

Rachel's influence has reached across the country through her teaching and choreographic work. In 1987-88 she was invited to be artist-in-residence in the Dance Department at Toronto's York University. Accompanied by Ben, she moved to Toronto, where she was active in the department teaching and creating. She met student dancer Andrea Nann at York and, recognizing her talent, remounted *Old Times Now* for her. This solo, which Rachel originally made with D-Anne Kuby, was widely performed. Rachel also created *In a Dark Time the Eye Begins to See*, one of her political dances, while she was at York University.

Patricia Fraser, a senior dancer and artistic director of the School of

Toronto Dance Theatre, was teaching at York University while Rachel was artist-in-residence. Fraser credits Rachel's example with helping many of the dance artists working at York maintain their artistic focus. She was able to keep her own priorities as an artist clear and not get side-tracked into the committee work and meetings which too often devour the energies of artists who work in academic settings.

Soon after the York University residency, Rachel asked Fraser to work with her. She created *Pat's Bach* for her. The dance is in seven sections. It was made to Glenn Gould's rendition of J.S. Bach's *Partita #5 in G Major*. The image is of a woman who needs to speak, who is trying to open her mouth and open her heart to speak. Fraser says this solo was her personal experience of a "bridge piece" from Rachel's earlier way of making dances. Fraser comments that Rachel was trying, as she often does in later dances, to create work which is more related to the spirit of the music than to its form. As well, *Pat's Bach* spoke of a particular time in the lives of both dancer and creator.

"Rachel was the lifeline to dance for me," recalls Fraser. An accomplished, mature performer, she was striking out into the hard path of the independent dance artist. *Pat's Bach* became part of a collection of works which Fraser presented on her solo program "Canadian Short Stories". *Pat's Bach* opened the program. Of the works on this program, says Fraser, this solo of Rachel's, the only one not created by commission, is the one which has led to a deepening, ongoing artistic relationship.

Rachel created a dance called *Sunset Sentences*, which premiered in May, 1989 in the fifth Festival of Canadian Modern Dance. This work appeared to be autobiographical, for it included three daughters, a grandmother and a mother. The characters in the dance drift and wander from one another, but they seem to be invisibly bonded. While the mother stays close to the grandmother, the three young women dance alone. The gestures seem to come right out of life. The grandmother stares straight ahead, while her daughter wheels her in her chair. The grandmother smooths the young women's hair and embraces her daughter.

A process of abstracting her life experience into art began to work through Rachel. She began to perceive her connection to artistic vitality through the expression of her own life issues. Although she does not consider *Sunset Sentences* one of her strongest dances, it stands out, along with the duet *Just About Us*, made for herself and Suzanne Oliver, as the first works that Rachel made which were overtly autobiographical. These dances were steps toward a direction which she would pursue later, for they started to put onstage what Rachel was living. But if she looked at *Sunset Sentences* in 1989, she saw only its limitations. By the time she started to create *Edgelit* in 1996, all the specifics had been stripped away.

A dancer with Contemporary Dancers recalls seeing Rachel's mother in the theatre during the very late 1980's. It was difficult and slow for Eva to get in and out of her chair, but Rachel continued to bring her to every performance. Eva was integral to Rachel's life and to the life of her family.

Eva lived alone until she was eighty-three. She lived on the third floor of a private home, near St. John's Park, where she would go to sit and face the sun and commune with the light and trees, as she had done all her life. When the owners of the house died, it was sold. Rachel convinced her mother to move to the house where she and Ben lived.

Rachel has always needed to find financial assistance to support the creation of her art. Over the years she has received many Canada Council grants—more than a dozen from 1967-1990—and many awards from the Manitoba Arts Council. In 1989 she received a Senior Arts Grant from the Canada Council. Along with a Manitoba Arts Council Choreographers' Presentation Grant, it enabled her to mount her retrospective, which celebrated Contemporary Dancers' 25th Anniversary. In 1990 she was the recipient of a Media Projects in Dance Grant from the Canada Council. In 1994 she was awarded a Senior Arts Grant from the Canada Council, which she used for the creation of her 1995 work *Toward Light*.

Rachel continues to give more than she gets back. It is not within her comprehension to do less than her utmost.

Hard Times and Changes at WCD

For Rachel, the final ignominy with Contemporary Dancers came after Tedd Robinson's departure in 1990. At the time he left, Rachel's relationship with the company was quite amicable. She continued to rehearse in the company and school studios and often taught in the school. She had autonomy and respect in the studio and was highly regarded by the company's administration for her success as a fundraiser. Despite her new directions as an independent, her ties to the company remained close.

When Robinson moved on to new artistic pursuits, Contemporary Dancers hired Charlie Moulton as artistic director. Moulton had many associations with the company, many ties and qualities which recommended him as a worthy candidate for the position.

He was the son of choreographer Robert Moulton, whose work was important in Contemporary Dancers' first years. Charlie had danced with Contemporary Dancers for the 1971 season, early in his career. Rachel remembers him as a very good dancer and a wonderful performer. He had enjoyed success as a dancer in New York, where he performed with the Merce Cunningham company. Acclaim for his choreography had gained him a reputation as a hot young post-modern dance artist. Rachel had invited him to set a work with Contemporary Dancers while she was directing the company. His dynamism and a certain continuity with the company made him a very attractive choice.

Once he was on the scene, it swiftly became apparent that Moulton had very definite ideas about what he wanted to see happen at Contemporary Dancers. Foremost in his mind was starting with a clean slate. His idea was to clear out the company's past in order to reinvigorate Contemporary Dancers.

As one of his first acts, Moulton announced that the company would be fundamentally reformed. Although the dancers who were members of the company had been told that their jobs were secure, Moulton had a different idea. The dancers discovered that they would be required to re-audition when he took over.

Few of the dancers did re-audition. For the most part those who were in the company when Moulton arrived were angry and affronted. Most of them decided to look elsewhere for work. Alana Shewchuk informed Moulton that it was her decision to go through the audition process, she was doing it for her own reasons. Then she opted to work elsewhere. Only one of the former company dancers, D-Anne Kuby, stayed on.

When Moulton decided to free up storage space by selling off costumes from Contemporary Dancers' earlier repertory, the school's directors acted quickly. They found room to house some of these artefacts of company history.

A condition of the contract which Moulton signed with Contemporary Dancers' board was that Rachel Browne, acknowledged since 1983 as the company's founding artistic director, was to be denied access to the company's studios. It is Rachel's understanding that Moulton undertook this condition to try to keep her influence, her presence and her history away from what he saw as a new day for the company.

Rachel was furious at this insult, but kept her anger under wraps. She defied this contractual agreement and continued to frequent the building, though she mostly worked in the school's space, in the spare studio, or at night, when the company studio was not in use. She had a show coming up and she needed the rehearsal space. Privately, she let it be known that if Moulton wanted to enforce the ban on her presence in the studios, she would have to be thrown out of the building. Defiantly, she called her 1990 season "Fine, Thank You!"

Rachel kept silence while Moulton began his first season with the company. It soon became apparent that artistic difficulties and grave financial problems were rapidly spiralling the company into a state of crisis. Karen Kuzak, a member of the company during Tedd Robinson's years as director, recalls how she and other former members of Contemporary Dancers felt. "We watched it end," she says, suggesting a shared apprehension about the company's fate. "We watched it end."

Gradually, Rachel began to let it be known that she had been ill-

treated by the company. The dance community has its own bush tele-
graph; word spread across the country.

Meanwhile, many of the board members had started looking askance
at Moulton's single-handed approach to running the company. Right
away, some of them had objected to his having required the dancers to
re-audition. Board members felt strongly that they should be involved
with decisions concerning work conditions for the dancers. Moulton
did not confer with the board about many of his aims. Communication
became a problem, as the company sped toward financial breakdown.

Moulton mounted a production in Winnipeg at the Walker Theatre
called *What is Love?* Many of the board members felt that it was not
very effective artistically. Here, Rachel says, she felt bound to disagree
with them, on the grounds that it was not the place of board members
to make artistic judgments.

By March of 1991 Rachel had had enough. She feared for the
company's survival. She went to the *Winnipeg Free Press* and blew the
whistle. She gave the newspaper the story of how Moulton's direction
was rapidly destroying the company. She made it known that Moulton
had threatened to lock the company's doors to her. Rachel also went to
the Canada Council and to the Manitoba Arts Council with this information.

Certain board members, led by Richard Irish and including Ellen
Oberlander and Nancy Botkin, were highly concerned about what was
happening. New to the board that year, their perspective about what
was occurring was fresh; they soon grew anxious to take steps to preserve
the integrity of the company.

The new board members felt very strongly that the treatment which
Rachel had received needed redress. Restoring the company's soundness,
they felt, meant re-establishing Rachel's status with the company. Rachel
received a telephone call from these board members, who wanted to
meet with her privately. Rachel's first response was to be very wary.
But she did speak with this "new guard". She recalls meeting them for
coffee in a Winnipeg restaurant. She was very guarded, suspicious of
their intentions. Eventually she became convinced of the sincerity of
their desire to reverse the company's trends. She was in discussion with
them about being reinstated to the company as an honourary lifetime
member of the board of directors when the board fired Moulton in the
spring of 1991.

Rachel felt that the board's desire to save the company was genuine. She began to do some voluntary fundraising for the company and agreed to be part of the committee which was to search for a new artistic director. It is clear that Rachel's continuing involvement with Contemporary Dancers was singularly important in saving the company from closure.

Charlie Moulton's short time with Contemporary Dancers had profound effects. It was very nearly the death of the company and sent the school into a spin. Quite quickly, Faye Thomson and Odette Heyn-Penner took a tight hold on the school's finances. They kept the school stable by cutting their spending radically so that the budget would balance.

A majority of the company dancers, many of whom had been trained in the school, dispersed in their search for work. Suddenly, they were seen dancing in Vancouver, Montreal, Toronto. The high calibre of their training and the range of their dancing were the best kind of advertisement for the school. This scattering effect was a factor, say the directors, in the school becoming better known across Canada.

The search for a new artistic director was long and difficult. Eventually the company hired choreographer Tom Stroud, who joined the company in the fall of 1991. Stroud has a diverse background in Canadian theatre and dance. He has danced with Karen Jamieson, with Toronto Independent Dance Enterprise, and in the work of Jean-Pierre Perreault. He is a noted choreographer, and a skilled, enthusiastic instigator of choreographic labs and cross-disciplinary projects. A new manager, Karen Johnson, briefly joined the company with the new artistic director. Quite soon, Alanna Keefe assumed the position of administrative director.

All the key staff in the school and company agreed to work for six months with no pay. This saved Contemporary Dancers from declaring bankruptcy. Though these personal subsidies saved the company from immediate closure, it was hard, recalls school director Faye Thomson wryly, to live down someone else's debt.

She and Heyn-Penner recognized that the time had come to declare the school's autonomy from the company. The school had grown up and needed to offer continuity to its students, rather than frequent, essential changes in aesthetic and style tied to changes "upstairs" in the company. Soon after Stroud's arrival the school incorporated separately from the company. Rachel continued to teach and act as a mentor in the school throughout this time.

Through the first months after he became artistic director, Stroud spent intensive amounts of time making long- and short-term plans for Contemporary Dancers. A thoughtful planner and a responsible artist, in taking on the company's direction, he took on its past and its future.

The company's situation was very precarious. Stroud speaks of Rachel being very helpful to him, in a most basic way, through this vulnerable time.

"I couldn't imagine letting the company go while Rachel was in this world. I don't think Rachel Browne could imagine it. She is a source of strength, everybody in the community feels that way. If you know Rachel, there's no griping, you just keep focused on the work and do it. You find a way."

Stroud has taken the company in new directions. He has worked very hard to place and sustain Contemporary Dancers as a vital part of the national dance community and as a lively participant in the animation of the local dance scene. Expectations for company partnerships with business and other artistic organizations are high. Artistic innovation is constantly considered. Many levels of artistic seniority and many levels of funding make up the national picture. Complexity and the stiff competition for money make finding innovative ways of operating a necessity.

Stroud has worked to put in place new models of residency and new initiatives for collaboration among mid-sized companies. The 1994 tour of Jean-Pierre Perreault's *Joe* is one example. Dancers from Contemporary Dancers, Dancemakers and La Fondation Jean-Pierre Perreault joined forces for a continent-wide tour of Perreault's milestone work. Stroud also has a concept of "double residencies", which gives companies the opportunity to do creation, tour to other cities, work with guest choreographers and network through expanded companies and opportunities.

Rachel and Stroud have not always seen eye to eye, but they have always maintained a workable connection. While Rachel admits that there has been some friction between them, she also sees that as inevitable. Over time they have evolved a relationship of respect; part of this is respect for one another's differences. Rachel always invites Stroud in to see a run-through of new work. He responds with thoughtful questions. He is respectful of Rachel's unshakable commitment to dance and of her deeply personal relationship to her art. He recognizes that dance continually enthralls her. For Rachel's part, she recognizes that, in certain ways, she is the past to him. She credits his point of view with at times helping her to take a new path herself.

Rachel's work was prominent in the company's retrospective 30th anniversary performances, given at the Gas Station Theatre from November 10 to 13, 1994. Excerpts of *Anerca* and *Contrasts* represented Rachel's early creation. Company dancer Olivia Thorvaldson performed "All My Trials", a solo from *Odetta's Songs and Dances* which was originally danced by Rachel herself. Professional program students danced "It's a Mighty World", the finale of *Odetta's Songs and Dances*. *Roz*, a work by Tedd Robinson, was presented on the program, as were Stephanie Ballard's 1980 work *Prairie Song* and her 1986 work *Prayer*, which was danced by Faye Thomson. Work by Odette Heyn-Penner was also performed. Stroud showed his 1990 work *The Fence*. The program concluded with Alana Shewchuk performing Rachel's 1992 work *Mouvement*. Reviewing the performance in the *Winnipeg Free Press*, writer Garth Bucholz called *Mouvement* "a thrillingly ingenious study of impulse and action, performed with feral vigor..."

Mentor, Creator

Certain works shine like beacons in the minds of their creators. Some germ of a new direction may emerge, surprising a creator, compelling her forward, sideways, or into an entirely new kind of perception. To Rachel, *Mouvement*, created with Alana Shewchuk in 1992, is such a work. The work marked breakthroughs for both the dancer and the choreographer.

For Shewchuk, the creation of *Mouvement* was a coming of age. She had suffered a broken foot and was returning to dancing after a year away when Rachel called to ask if she would work with her. She was reluctant at first, knowing Rachel's need to see full dancing in rehearsal. She also knew that she had to pace herself carefully to avoid re-injury. Rachel assured her that the dancing would not be taxing, that she would be able to manage it.

Mouvement is spare and animalistic, radical for Rachel. It marked the beginning of a whole new phase for her, a years-long investigation of what she calls "raw" or "animal" movement. Her art finally came out. It was fundamentally through a change in tempo. Rachel's work has a rhythmic heart. In making *Mouvement*, she just slowed down. Rachel did not allow herself her usual responses, her usual musicality, her usual preparedness. She just wanted to see… She credits Shewchuk, who was willing to trust her, to go as far as needed, for the creative discoveries of *Mouvement*.

During the process of making the dance, Rachel brought an image to rehearsal. It was Mexican painter Frida Kahlo's painting of a wounded deer, image of a wild feminine vulnerability. Thinking of the creation of this work, which was so important to her, Rachel reflects that she found a "creatureliness". Previously she had made several attempts to shed her customary ways of choreographing. This time, she was willing to try the rawest, most basic movement, anything that could get her to a new point of departure.

Mouvement has had many effects. Dancer and choreographer Davida Monk recalls seeing *Mouvement* on videotape. Shortly after seeing it, she encountered Rachel. Struck by the impact of *Mouvement,* even on video, she approached Rachel, who she did not know well at the time, to offer her dancing skills.

Davida Monk calls *Mouvement* "an enormous revelation" for Rachel choreographically. She compares the level of artistic discovery to that of Nijinsky's dances—organic, provoking a way of taking the work in as an experience rather than as a veneer of performance. Monk connected right away to the head and heart of Rachel's work. She has become a core participant in creating and performing Rachel's dances. First in *Four Haiku,* then in *Toward Light* and more recently in *Edgelit,* she has been involved in the long evolution of directions that have followed Rachel's animalistic phase.

Mouvement also brought Rachel serious attention as a creator elsewhere. For the very first time in all her years of creating and staging dance a number of her colleagues and peers told her they liked a dance of hers. Karen Kuzak, then a member of Contemporary Dancers, remembers seeing *Mouvement,* excitedly thinking, "This is really good," and craving an opportunity to dance the work herself.

Rachel has come full circle in certain ways. In Contemporary Dancers' early days, she booked the company. As an independent choreographer, she continues to seek opportunities to show her work.

In 1992 Rachel was invited to participate in the INDE festival. These Toronto festivals, brainchild of dancer/choreographer/instigator Terrill Maguire, paired choreographers and composers for the creation of original work. Rachel made *Dreamrite* for INDE, with Winnipeg composer Diana McIntosh. Although Rachel calls the work "a bomb," she was experimenting in the work, a ritualistic dance for five women and could see a seed of something. She never developed it to her own satisfaction, even after re-working it five times.

Without a company, presenting work can be a quandary for a senior artist. Rachel, not surprisingly, enjoys the democratic process of acceptance to a fringe festival; it is consistent with her ideas of equality and equal access.

"Sending work to Dancing on the Edge, which is curated, or to fFIDA… I love to do this and I like to present my work in a low-risk situation. I was able to get some intelligent reviews, which is a great gift. I really like the democratic process by which one got into a fringe festival. I felt that there was certainly a place for a format like that. I remember Grant Strate saying, 'You're not going to get contaminated by bad work. Don't worry about it, it will just fall by the wayside. And the good work will shine through.' I like mixed programs with novice choreographers with some more experienced people. It's very interesting to see. I'm not worried by the fact that some of it is lousy."

It is not easy for Rachel to "pitch" her work. It is not cutting edge dance, and producers, who hold a good deal of control in Canada over which artists get seen where, are often looking for the latest, hottest, newest. Nonetheless, Rachel does get invitations.

For several years Rachel was part of a loosely structured Winnipeg collective called "Three Square Pegs". Budding choreographers Sharon Moore, Constance Cooke, a Ryerson University dance program graduate, and Rachel shared dancers and resources to mount programs for the Winnipeg fringe festivals. Rachel liked showing her work on a program with two younger choreographers; they generally showed new work while she showed works which had already been created. Three Square Pegs presented their mixed programs for several editions of the fringe festivals, managing to engender some "festival fever", as Moore recalls. Rachel recollects that their programs attracted "huge audiences" and that they actually made some money from these performances.

When her name has been drawn in the lottery by which presenters at Toronto's annual fringe Festival of Independent Dance Artists (fFIDA) are selected, Rachel has shown her work there. Since 1991, her work has found very favourable critical response in fFIDA showings. In 1991 she presented *Pat's Bach* and *Freddy*, which was danced by Moore. Dance writer Alina Gildner noted in *The Globe and Mail* on August 10, 1991, "Each is a solo for an exceptional dancer…and each is new for the festival. The first has a very trapped, pained and introspective quality, driven by Bach's "Partita #5 in G Major." And the second is a hard-edge view of broken-heartedness, set to Teresa Stratas's recording of

Kurt Weill songs. Each is an elegant, strong piece of choreography, superbly performed."

Rachel premiered her work *Sharonblue*, for Moore, at fFIDA in 1992. Moore recalls this as the work in which she "got into Rachel's groove" and could fully inhabit Rachel's sense of an inner impulse driving the dance. Reviewing these performances, Toronto arts journalist Michael Crabb wrote in *Dance Connection*, "In *Sharonblue*, [Rachel Browne] plumbs her chosen Cole Porter songs with movement that is always fresh and visceral, dynamically varied and emotionally intense."

In 1993, Rachel presented an excerpt of *Four Haiku* at fFIDA. Reviewer Paula Citron found the work "...really, really beautiful, very deep and very rich..." In 1994, Rachel staged *K.J.3* at the festival. In the 1996 edition of fFIDA, she showed Davida Monk's *Toward Light* solo and Sharon Moore danced *My Romance*. Rachel's *Edgelit* solo for Lisa Kuhn was presented in the 1998 edition of fFIDA at Buddies in Bad Times theatre in downtown Toronto. In *The Globe and Mail* of August 21, 1998, journalist Finbarr O'Reilly commented, "Kuhn delivered an intense performance in which each detailed movement contained an essence and depth that was matched note for note by the musical score."

Other venues have also been a forum for Rachel's work. In 1992 Sharon Moore performed *Freddy* at the Canada Dance Festival. As well as showing her work at the Winnipeg Fringe Festival, Rachel has presented her dances at the Women in View Festival at Vancouver's Firehall Theatre. On a DanceWorks Mainstage program in April, 1993, at Toronto's Betty Oliphant Theatre, she showed *Freddy* (1991), which was danced by Moore, *Old Times Now* (1987), danced by Andrea Nann, and *Mouvement* (1992), which was performed by Alana Shewchuk. Journalist Paula Citron, commenting about this "string of virtuostic solos for gifted women performers" in the *Toronto Star*, noted, "For Browne, dance is a movement language that dialogues with music. Her dancers shudder, convulse, stamp, jump and angle their body parts as they convey a central idea in opposition to the melody line or rhythm."

In 1994, Rachel danced *Shalom* with Pat Fraser at *The Dance Goes On*, a gala performance at Toronto's Premiere Dance Theatre. Fraser has performed her work *Pat's Bach* in various Toronto venues. Rachel presented a complete evening of work at Dancers' Studio West in Calgary in 1997.

She has made two dances, *Re-tuning, or The Great Canadian Hoedown* (1995), set to Ann Southam's *Re-tuning*, and her potent dance *K.J.3* (1994), set to music by Keith Jarrett, as commissions for Toronto's Canadian Children's Dance Theatre. These works have been performed many times since by the company, which reaches a broad range of audience members through its family-oriented programming. This is significant to Rachel, for she aspires to a wider viewing of her work than it generally receives. At the heart of it, she is making dances with the hope that they will communicate. Having Rachel choreograph and teach for the Canadian Children's Dance Theatre is significant for artistic director Deborah Lundmark too, closing the circle of her long relationship with Rachel.

Creatively, a whole new phase started for Rachel with *Mouvement*. Somehow this work liberated her conceptually. There seems to be a parallel to the evolution of the work of visual artist Betty Goodwin. Always an artist, Goodwin's path of artistic truth brought her notice rather later than usual in her career. The scale and concept of her subjects all aligned, creating art of great visceral force. Goodwin's mature work seems to come out of a neural power, as if she is seeing through all the nerves of her body, not just through her eyes. Bodies have a density, an opacity that is at once intensely physical and universal. Goodwin's work is based on the body; images of bodies bent or supported by one another, images of vulnerability and pain. There is an accord, in this radical physicality, with Rachel's later work.

Rachel continues to look to nature as a source of inspiration. She spends some part of every day contemplating nature, a personal meditation which renews and stimulates her feelings of wanting to create movement. There is a place by the Red River, close to her house, where she goes in all seasons, even in winter, when the river is frozen, when the temperature drops to -35 and Winnipeggers are warned to stay indoors.

"I imagine the movement of the water," she says. "I have a favourite tree that I always look at…It's a place where I used to sit with my mother. I keep watching the currents and thinking that I could some-how imitate them, or remember them in my body, in my dances."

Rachel's last large group dances for some time were *Dreamrite*, cre-ated for INDE '92, and *In a Dark Time the Eye Begins to See*, her seventh version of the work she began at York University. A whole cycle of works related to the movement research she began with *Mouvement* carried Rachel through the mid-1990's. These tended to be smaller in scale than previous dances. Solos have always been a satisfying form for Rachel to work with. She loves delving, going as far as she can go with one dancer, one idea.

Rachel's mother moved to a personal care home in Winnipeg, the Sharon Home, in 1990. Her presence in Ben and Rachel's home became diffi-cult for Ben, who was retired and around the house a good deal. Rachel wanted only harmony, but with a heavy heart helped her mother move.

Eva had always found ways to support Rachel while doing what she felt was right as well. If Rachel, as she ran out the door to go on tour, admonished her mother not to buy grapes or lettuce from California, in support of striking workers, she knew her mother would do that very thing the moment she was gone. Eva had her ways of going silent, resisting Rachel's attempts to choreograph her behaviour. She called Rachel "The General". She had nicknames for the girls too. Ruth was "Ferocious", Miriam was "The Dutch Girl", for her blonde girlhood hair, always cut with straight bangs. And Annette was "snot-nose," the baby. Rachel's first husband Don had maintained a relation-ship with Eva. A social worker at the Mount Carmel Clinic, he used to visit every week at a certain time and spend time with her.

During Eva's last months, Rachel, Annette and Eva were a unit. They did not want anyone else present. "We went through a profound experience," recalls Annette, "with my Granny's death."

Rachel was involved with two sets of performances in the autumn of 1993. One was a performance of her own works in mid-October, the other was WCD's 30th anniversary celebrations. During the first performances, Rachel was onstage in her work *Continuum*. Her mother was dying as she danced. Rachel remembers thinking of her while she was onstage, speaking to her in Yiddish in her thoughts and feeling how appropriate the dance was. Her feelings fit with the voice of the solo cello in the Bach score.

Rachel says, "My mother was extremely loving and generous and completely self-sacrificing for the sake of what I needed." Eva died at the age of ninety-four, on October 31, 1993. Rachel remembers thinking, "My mother waited, so I could carry on with my dance."

≈   ≈   ≈

Rachel went through a transformation in her creative process with *Four Haiku*. Earlier, she always started preparing for weeks or months before beginning rehearsal with the dancers. As well as reading and thinking about the work, she started creating movement. She worked by herself in a studio to master a certain number of movements or phrases. This was a kind of security. Inevitably, once the rehearsal process was under way, things would change. But a more organic, less structured way of creating evolved for her.

With the creation of *Four Haiku*, Rachel made the decision to work only with women dancers. The dance, structured as four intertwined, intersecting solos, featured Sharon Moore, Pat Fraser, Davida Monk and Alana Shewchuk, artists of maturity and experience. Rachel and these dancers understand one another. It is difficult, says Rachel, to find men who dance and have a comparable maturity. By the early 1990's, depth of communication with dancers had become key to Rachel's creative process. Rachel became certain of her desire to work with women in order to make statements about herself as a woman choreographer. It was her desire, too, to speak about women dancing together, as well as about communication with women composers and other women artists.

Rachel chose the themes for her haiku—earth, wind, trees, water.

As preparation for *Four Haiku*, she did a great deal of improvising, giving herself themes or challenges to work on in the studio. She also improvised in her home, in the kitchen, in her living room and in the bedroom her mother had once occupied, which was still suffused with her presence. Rachel often takes writing, which she transforms into emotional, moving imagery, to this room. She calls it her "magic room". Bare of furniture, it is a small room on the second floor of her house, with a view of treetops and a certain ambiance.

Rachel did not videotape these improvisation sessions, but made notes about the texture and quality of movement discoveries she was making. Pat Fraser's solo, she recalls, came powerfully from movement originated in her mother's room.

Rachel also decided to work without music. She thought perhaps her deep love and respect for music, the pull of music, was holding her back choreographically. She thought she needed to take her next step forward in silence, and decided to work with just the bare elements of movement. She would take the risk that anything could happen. She set aside her old process, going into rehearsal by preparing herself emotionally, ready to work improvisationally, and with a general idea of what she was working for.

She loved the results. She rehearsed the work's solos independently. When the four dancers came together for the first time, she played with ideas about overlapping their dances. Rachel is fascinated by the potential of such juxtaposition to create new currents and subtleties within a dance. For the dancers, it opened a new area of awareness. It was the beginning, perhaps, of a change in the way that Rachel perceives time.

Dancer Pat Fraser related to the work as poetic rather than theatrical. Fraser took detailed notes when rehearsing and creating with Rachel. The work was so deeply image-based, she explained, that if you lost the image, you lost the movement. In *Four Haiku* the instructions from Rachel were all either images, or action-oriented—push, stagger, stumble, fall, scream. Images and verbs catalysed movement.

Rachel found the dancers of *Four Haiku* to be sublime, their performances enriched by their belief in the work. She particularly cherishes images of Sharon Moore's dance, "water". The dancer becomes water, nearly drowning, in the imagery of this solo. Choreographically, Rachel tried to have Moore capture the movement of water. From wading to being engulfed, from birth to drowning, Rachel found the metaphor of a lifeline through this solo.

"I keep on coming back to dances about the life cycle in some form. Birth, death, renewal. My mother was dying at the same time and though I didn't incorporate that consciously, it was there. I saw it so clearly when I looked afterwards. When the dance was finally formed she appeared all over the place. It felt like a major cathartic experience. I thought the dancers were magnificent. They were giving everything, and had such belief in it."

Four Haiku premiered at the Gas Station Theatre in late October, 1993, the second half of a program Rachel called *Cameos*. The evening included earlier works, *Continuum*, a work from 1990, *For David*, made in 1991, and *My Romance*, dating from 1990. Journalist Garth Buchholz, commenting on the program in the *Winnipeg Free Press*, wrote, "Seven dance artists, including Browne herself, gave passionate, breathtaking interpretations of choreography that blended muscular physicality with an almost unsettling vulnerability." Browne's works, he wrote, particularly mentioning *Four Haiku*, "fearlessly summon the most poignant emotions."

Rachel feels *Mouvement* and *Four Haiku* to be related in spirit and connected choreographically. Although she was not deliberately striving to be experimental, she considers that she did move forward at an essential level in both works. This elemental shift occurred, she feels, through a chemistry of complete commitment on the part of the dancers and the workings of her altered choreographic process.

෨   ෨   ෨

In 1995 Rachel presented *Toward Light*, her first evening-length work. *Toward Light* gathered eleven performers, all women of varying ages, from young student dancers to Rachel herself.

Toward Light was the culmination of her investigation of basic drives and urges and of instinctual, raw, almost animal-like movement. She wanted to create "wild, free, non-derivative rhythmic phrases". She dealt with images of breaking through and grasping. A mute dignity in the dancers' intense efforts was often difficult to watch. The dancing was spare and fiercely focused. The dancers speak of the absolute attention which was necessary to perform the work.

Rachel came to a place within *Toward Light* where she was concerned with capturing intangibles, subtle currents of feeling and fugitive thoughts. Feeling the restrictiveness of being drawn by music, she responded to what she has called the "special challenge" of creating in silence and finding appropriate music later. The music she chose for *Toward Light* was a commissioned score for solo piano by Ann Southam, and Rachel's beloved Bach, the *Fifth Suite for Violoncello in C minor*, as played by Dutch cellist Anner Bylsma.

The program note for *Toward Light* read, "While movement exploration is at the core of the dance, some of the images I use are inspired by the book *Women Who Run With the Wolves: Myths and Stories of the Wild Woman Archetype* by Clarissa Pinkola Estes. R.B."

Rachel collaborated with Winnipeg artist Agnetha Dyck on the production of *Toward Light*. Dyck was creating work with bees at the time. By placing articles of women's apparel—clothing or shoes, for instance—into beehives, she encouraged the bees to start to build comb on these items. Their structures were altered by the bees' work on them, creating a kind of sculpture in progress. The results were very strange and wonderful—a cross-cultural exchange between the insect world and the human world. In *Toward Light*, the beework pieces on the stage symbolized the instinctual matter with which Rachel was dealing, a not-quite-human expression.

Davida Monk opened *Toward Light* with a taut solo performed in silence. From the inside of her dance, she describes a sensation of being emphatically physically engaged. Performing her solo meant working with a great deal of muscular contraction, embodying the physical tensions which conveyed the metaphor of the work.

Karen Kuzak, returning to Winnipeg after dancing with Le Groupe de La Place Royale and O Vertigo, heard that Rachel was creating a new work. She called Rachel to say that she needed to be in it, and Rachel responded to this dancerly need. Her *Toward Light* solo, reflects Kuzak, empowered her to go on with the next steps she was to take in her life. "I desperately needed," Kuzak recalls, "to be in the studio with Rachel; I needed something for me." Her solo was a "warrior woman", aggressive, with much jumping and posturing, imparting a strong sense of attack and retreat. She worked with one image of biting a pear off a tree, another of peeling off her skin. A key image in her solo was of her breasts as eyes, scanning the environment.

The lack of music in the first solo of *Toward Light*, and later in the work, was somewhat arduous for the audience. It is as though Rachel perceives the dancer as music, a rhythmic presence with the power to shape time through phrasing and gesture. Her point of departure is the completeness of the dancer and the dance. One does not expect music to augment a sculpture or a painting; perhaps it is Rachel's way of insisting on an absence of distractions from looking at the essence of the dance.

Toward Light was made up of six dances which followed one another seamlessly. Four solos, for Davida Monk, Alana Shewchuk, Karen Kuzak and Pat Fraser, a duet for Odette Heyn-Penner and Sharon Moore, and a final duet for Heyn-Penner and Rachel Browne were the spine of the work. A quartet of young dancers wove around and through the hour-long work, during Alana Shewchuk's solo and during the last duet. At the end they were highlighted, vital, young, strong, taking the work on.

Many people found *Toward Light* disturbing. Rachel's daughters found it hard to watch the angst of the work. Annette associates the work with the anguish that she and her mother shared while Rachel's mother was dying. So while she enjoyed the last dance of the work, she reacted strongly to other sections and found Moore's solo extremely painful to watch. Davida Monk says her partner can not bear to watch her perform the bleak, groping solo which opens the work. He wants to pull her off the stage, out of that place of extreme despair.

Rachel, after the work was created, reflected that she found *Toward Light* flawed. Ann Southam declared herself unsatisfied with the music she wrote. Nonetheless, *Toward Light* was a watershed achievement for Rachel.

Intense scrutiny of women's inner impulses has developed as a source of Rachel's work. The way in which she works with dancers is inextricably woven with her explorations.

Pat Fraser, a long-time collaborator, notes that Rachel encourages a dialogue with dancers, allowing the dancer to pursue a line of thought or a physical direction, whether it follows her original choreographic intention or not. Rachel, says Davida Monk, sets a broad context within which she trusts the dancer. There is room and time for the dancer to discover the dance and this allows a tremendous sense of liberation. Rachel rarely demonstrates. She might say, "Go deep. Move your body sideways, as though you're trying to struggle."

Many of the dancers Rachel worked with in making *Toward Light* say that steps and positions have little to do with the work; it is gestural, physical imagery. Dancers have to come to the work, minimal though it is, with full physical and emotional involvement. Every rehearsal feels like a full-out run; working with Rachel, dancers feel that there is no reason to mark movement. Seeing her work danced with full commitment is extremely important to Rachel's choreographic eye. She demands the very best of the performer, comments Karen Kuzak, and then asks for a little more.

Monk says that her experiences of working with Rachel have been illuminating about the source of Rachel's dance. Shape, she says, is not the primary issue. The work is connected with honing shape, but not made for the sake of external shape. She might give an example, "Hold your hands as if you are playing the piano." Movement is not from the outside, but from the exact moment of internal impulse.

Dancer Sharon Moore speaks of a shared trust in the rehearsal process. Rachel is willing to let the dance reveal itself to her. Her trust and acuity allow her and the dancers to be involved at a dynamic artistic level. Moore credits her work with Rachel on *Toward Light* with inspiring a personal realization about performing and creating. Simply, it is the idea that there is always more than one thing going on. Moore finds that the idea of the complex resonance of physical and emotional nuances in every moment has provided her access to a powerful depth in performance. It is an elusive ideal.

Moore credits Rachel's extraordinary artistic breakthroughs to her ability to see things through, not skirt issues or go around them, but face them and move through to a new level. She recalls a near-telepathic rapport with Rachel during the making of *Toward Light*. She had a sense that ideas and emotional nuances were being transferred from Rachel to her without the need to say a great deal. She found this sense of intuitive connection wonderfully satisfying. Through it, Rachel seeks to speak about the soul in her dances.

Rachel's sources are always acknowledged. They are often deep background, at the level of research. Whether text, image or music, Rachel lets the sources distill; over time, it seems, she has found the way to trust that her unconscious, and the craft she has amassed over decades of dancing, watching and making dance, will come together. She takes the essence of the metaphor she wants to use and extends it.

Rachel's daughter Miriam says she is floored by her mother's occasional, casual comments about movement sources. She might ask Miriam, who is a knitter, "Did you see the knitting?" Miriam, for her part, is completely baffled and amazed that the abstraction which characterizes her mother's dances could have a literal source.

But despite the close communication with dancers, Rachel is the creator. She is a distant, but clear guide. She is the director. The dance comes through her, with a sense of alertness to the dancers' input and experiences, and a sense of openness to change. Movement may be awkward or minimal, but if they are fully engaged with it, dancers have the experience that the movement informs them about the dance. There is always the sense that Rachel relates to the physical difficulty, the effort of dancing, as a metaphor in and of itself.

She is very demanding. Dancers work very hard for her. She will always ask to see one more run-through, one more time. She once chastised a dancer for not showing up to rehearsal when the young woman had been flat on her back for two weeks with mononucleosis.

One seasoned dancer describes how Rachel asked her, pregnant and exhausted, her back aching, to do one more run-through of a duet which she and Rachel were rehearsing. She resorted to saying, "Yes, Rachel, but I need you to do it with me." Rachel obligingly joined the dance. Her drained partner, aware that Rachel takes her glasses off to dance, was able to satisfy Rachel while for once dancing less than full-out, knowing that Rachel could not see her very well. But it is a fine line. Dancers respect Rachel for this relentless quality.

A friend called Rachel's home, concerned about her health at a time when she was very ill. She was still too weak to come to the telephone, reported Ben, but she was getting up and coming downstairs to do her class every day. Such discipline has been part of Rachel's life since childhood. She expects dedication beyond all from other dancers too.

While Rachel plays down recognition of her achievements, shrugging them off, acknowledgment continues to come her way. In 1995 she was the recipient of the Jean A. Chalmers Award for Creativity in Dance, a national, lifetime award of great prestige. Acknowledgment comes; but the work itself is always the main thing for Rachel.

Following the creation of *Toward Light*, Rachel's work altered again. With *Six Messages* and *Edgelit*, the work has become increasingly organic. These are no longer "pieces", per se, separate from one another, but aspects or stages which Rachel explores. Although she has always reworked and reconsidered her dances, her commitment to this artistic process has changed. Her present process is reminiscent of phases in a painter's career, like Georgia O'Keeffe's periods painting flowers or animal skulls. This is familiar enough in visual art, but most unusual in dance.

With *Six Messages*, Rachel found herself drawn to more refined movement, a minimal approach to gesture. Thoughtful, controlled, contained, the dances revolve around the slow passage of time. They seem to be works which explore the essential nature of time—stage time, real time, dream time, memory time.

This cycle of work has marked a new phase of collaboration with composer Ann Southam. Southam's music is "what I want to dance about," says Rachel. It has a vibrant simplicity, lucidity, at times a quality of transparency. The music is evocative without being descriptive. Hearing Southam's pieces "Fluke Sound" and "Music for Slow Dancing" spurred Rachel's thinking, initiating the creation of *Edgelit* and *Six Messages*.

Rachel describes listening to this music with Southam for the first time in February of 1996. Composer and choreographer sat in two chairs, facing one another obliquely, the sound system between them in the middle of the room. They listened to the electronic music, which is full of huge acoustic spaces. It was toward evening, the daylight gradually fading. Rachel recalls being aware of what she was thinking, of what the composer's thoughts were, of the two chairs. Southam commented, "It feels as if the heartbeat slows down."

This was the beginning—the two women, the hushed atmosphere, the chairs. The music is completely repetitive; haunting and hypnotic, it conjures for Rachel a time and place that has always been there. This set of circumstances became the core imagery of *Six Messages*, a polarity, two sides being continually drawn toward one another.

Rachel was due to make a work in the professional program at the school of Contemporary Dancers. She decided to use this electronic score of Southam's. She began working with the students. The dance streamed out. "It was as if," she recalls happily, "it could keep coming out endlessly." The movement was gradual and slow, then spiked with bursts of energy and emotion before receding back to a slow pace. Rachel describes the making of *Six Messages* as "euphoric". She felt absolutely attuned to its creation. The dance felt "right", true to her inner experience. It was a surprise, a relief, to create this slow work; as though she had found a precisely meditative pace, a spontaneous inner flow of presence, activity and creativity.

The dancers, Rachel recalls, responded to her intense interest in the connectedness she felt. They could feel her clarity and it inspired them. When *Six Messages* was first performed at the Gas Station Theatre, with Southam in the audience, there was a hush in the hall. *Six Messages* has an ambiance of entrancement.

After working with Rachel on the presentation of *Toward Light*, Davida Monk asked Rachel to create a solo for her. Rachel was drawn to return to the material of *Six Messages*, developing it further with Monk. The work became *Edgelit*, named after a poem by Adrienne Rich. They worked together in the summer of 1996, when Rachel was teaching at the University of Calgary, where Monk is on the faculty.

During the floods which threatened Winnipeg in the spring of 1997, Rachel travelled with five dancers to Calgary to present a program of her work. Monk had already performed the *Edgelit* solo in Calgary, so for this program Rachel put together her solo and three dancers, once again re-working the material of *Six Messages*. Rachel called this imprint of the work *Four Messages*. On this program as well were *K.J.3*, *My Romance* and the twenty-three minute finale section of *Toward Light*.

On their return from these performance dates, Odette Heyn-Penner recalls, Rachel's husband Ben was waiting to pick them up at the Winnipeg airport. Winnipeg was in crisis, sandbagging furiously, with the help of the armed forces, waiting for the flood to recede. Meeting Rachel and the dancers, Ben asked, "Is the river half-full or half-empty?"

Rachel dresses for action. Generally, she wears sweatpants, a T-shirt and a pair of sneakers. She is quite uninterested in fashion.

Rachel received a letter informing her that she was to be awarded the Order of Canada in the summer of 1997. She was disconcerted. The invitation indicated that evening wear was appropriate for the investiture ceremony and suggested long dresses for women. Rachel telephoned her regrets. She was sorry, she said, she could not attend and she did not wear dresses. Not being in agreement with the politics of the government of the day, she felt quite ambivalent about the award. Also, she felt that there were many, many deserving artists who were not to be so honoured.

Ruth pressed her mother to attend the event. Rachel's Winnipeg daughters Ruth and Miriam outfitted her for the event, helping her choose a pair of elegant trousers and a jacket. Rachel admits that she looked "very nice" in her medal-receiving outfit. She was permitted to bring one guest and Ruth accompanied her to Ottawa.

Travelling to the investiture was illuminating for Ruth. She describes seeing her mother there, for the first time in her life, as a person of national stature. There were crowds of notable people at Rideau Hall, many clamouring to meet and talk with Rachel. Ruth had a vivid sense of her mother's five decades of discipline and achievement—as a ballerina, as the originator of Winnipeg's Contemporary Dancers, as an artistic director, as a teacher, as founder of the WCD school, as a modern dancer, as a choreographer and as the the creator of a significant body of work. In this context Ruth was struck in a new way by her mother's complete humility and by her continuing commitment to dance.

Rachel was happy, in the end, that she decided to go to the investiture. She enjoyed the opportunity to meet many of the remarkable women who were receiving the Order of Canada that day. She was especially proud to share the event with Ruth.

Rachel has journeyed to a cabin at Willow Island, at the northern end of Lake Winnipeg, every summer for many years. In the summer of 1997, she sat and read and thought by the lake, torn by deep personal change. On her return to Winnipeg she worked with the professional program students at Contemporary Dancers' school. She made a joyful dance for them called *Willow Island* which she set to music by The Penguin Café Orchestra.

One day in rehearsal the students were not responding to direction in quite the way that Rachel needed to see. She sat down with them and started to tell them about some of the things she was going through. She could see tears in their eyes, and heard her own voice getting shaky. But afterward, she could see that the conversation had moved them toward a new understanding of how to dance her work.

Students love Rachel's genuineness. Odette Heyn-Penner says the fourth-year students always ask her when they will have the opportunity to work with Rachel, as they know that she has a special touch. They know that she will ask a great deal of them and they want to be challenged as only Rachel can challenge. They recognize her artistry, her fairness, her wise eyes, and her demanding nature, as what they need. They see, says Heyn-Penner, what Rachel can draw out of young dancers. They want to be pushed in that way. The directors perceive that Rachel appreciates diligence, and see her desire to take things as far as they can go.

Faye Thomson comments that Rachel sees potential in dance students perhaps before they see it themselves. She can see what they are capable of in the future and how they can develop. Seeing potential in a dancer, Rachel will go after some quality or achievement from her and not give up until she gets it.

Her clarity is valued. Heyn-Penner says she loves watching Rachel rehearse her work with the students. She'll cry and laugh and dance a whole dance in her chair. She gives detailed notes without writing a single note—she lives the work. Heyn-Penner comments that she has never been in a rehearsal process with Rachel that didn't unfold quite naturally.

Rachel handed responsibility to the school's directors when they were very young. It is an exemplary foundation for the school. The directors' devoted capability has fully borne out her intuitive faith in their potential. Both Thomson and Heyn-Penner honour Rachel as their mentor. They welcome her continuing presence in the school, where she is acknowledged founding artistic director.

In December, 1997, the School of Contemporary Dancers celebrated its 25th anniversary. The directors planned a gala celebration. The performances were sold out for four nights at the Gas Station Theatre. Many, many audience members were there to see Rachel.

Thomson and Heyn-Penner had to press Rachel to perform. It seemed perfectly appropriate to them that she should appear on the stage. Rachel was very reluctant, but they "dragged her, kicking and screaming" onto the stage. "We insisted," they say. "We learned it from her."

Rachel performed her work *Toward Light* with Heyn-Penner. In this duet she is carried onstage on the younger dancer's back. Heyn-Penner cherished the intensity of moments she shared onstage with Rachel in these performances. She remarks that Rachel is completely comfortable with who she is and what she does, and in this way is a source of guidance to those around her. In these performances of *Toward Light*, Rachel was onstage with absolute honesty, not trying to be a dancer that she is not.

In the gala program, Heyn-Penner and Thomson paid a special thank you to Rachel, "who is always there to support and encourage and sometimes push".

The professional program students danced *Willow Island*. Afterward, Rachel said, many of them came to her. "We love it when you cry watching us perform," they said. "We know you love the way we dance." The school's directors comment on the way in which Rachel connected the youth of the students with the natural beauty of the island. This is a kind of grace. In times of great personal turmoil, Rachel has often been able to create a danced ambiance of honesty, serenity and beauty.

෧   ෧   ෧

Edgelit has become a cycle of work which continues to fascinate Rachel and draw her on creatively. Parallel with the creation of this pliant vehicle has come personal change. The work is Rachel's metaphor for profound shifts in her life. She says that *Edgelit* has revealed to her how she was feeling, in a very passionate way.

Rachel has changed her life in order to live in the community of women.

"I've always considered myself a really strong feminist," says Rachel, "an ardent, radical feminist. And it was that awareness, along with many life occurrences, that pushed me further in this direction."

She and Ben Sokoloff live in different cities now. They separated in the early spring of 1998. Separation and a new path have been painful for Rachel in a way which was impossible for her to foresee. The path is by no means clear. Yet no one is suprised by her changes. She moves ahead with the full knowledge and support of her family.

Her daughter Miriam says Rachel is radical with her own life, that she is evolved and evolving. She expects her mother to be on the edge in her thinking, as well as in her work. "She is a person of change."

Her eldest, Ruth, says Rachel makes no excuses or compromises for the tough issues she takes on. Many of these have had to do with her political stands and with issues around young people and women. Her mother, she says, relates to struggle. She encourages others to fight from a position of strength. "I think," says Ruth, "that's what a lot of her work is about."

෧   ෧   ෧

In January of 1997, while teaching in Toronto, Rachel worked once again with Pat Fraser, creating another *Edgelit* solo, this time using Ann

Southam's "Fluke Sound".

Southam had played "Soundstill", a work for piano, for Rachel during the summer of 1996. Hearing the work had an intense effect on Rachel. She continued to listen to Southam's music, finding a source of calm, a meditative quality in the piano score. She used this music in her work with Lisa Kuhn, the graduating student in the professional program for whom she created the third *Edgelit* solo. She speaks of Kuhn's amazing instinct for understanding what is underneath and all around a gesture. She is remarkable, says Rachel, a magician, able to conjure up a world of emotion and imagery onstage.

In June 1998, with assistance from the Manitoba Arts Council, Rachel gave a studio showing of her work on *Edgelit* to that point. She showed the solo for Kuhn, the solo for Pat Fraser and a quartet made of the solo for Davida Monk combined with the trio. She was very satisfied with this studio event. There was an "installation" feeling about the way the work could be looked at, regarded in plain daylight. Rachel felt very relaxed about the presentation. Southam attended, as did many of Rachel's friends and colleagues—everyone was there because of personal connection to Rachel. Afterward, the dancers and Rachel went out to share a meal, lingering and laughing together for a long time. Then they drove out to The Forks, the riverside park at the confluence of the Red and Assiniboine Rivers, to walk in the early summer evening.

Rachel was happy. It is rare to look at one's work and feel that it is good and seen in the right place.

What is the fascination for Rachel of these chairs and the women? Her description of the whole cycle of *Edgelit* is "a gradual unfolding of longing".

In part it is a longing for acknowledgment of who she is and who she is becoming. It is a longing to satisfy her own eye, and all that she sees. Looking at a woman dancer, says Rachel, a woman of maturity and experience standing by a chair, is so much about the woman who is dancing. She is not just standing there. Everything she has lived is standing there. Everything she brings to the moment will communicate. The movement and emotional choices tell an inner story, express an inner motion and give it a reality.

Rachel treats dancers with equal respect. She enjoys working with younger dancers, as she did in *Toward Light* and *Edgelit*. As a result, notes Pat Fraser, the younger members of the "company" with whom Rachel is working at any given time feel free to assume their full selves. They can breathe and feel at liberty to enter the creative process in a climate of equality. Working outside the formality and expectations of a company frees Rachel to hand-pick dancers whose work inspires her.

In *Edgelit*, Rachel's socialism, her feminism and her art come together. With *Edgelit*, it seems there are no distances between idea and action for her. Respect and equality set the tone for the work.

Ann Southam felt that the meeting of music and dance in Kuhn's *Edgelit* solo was "wonderfully successful". Pat Fraser's solo was engaging to her for the way in which dance gestures were similar to musical phrases. Although the dance was not lined up with the music, there was an accord between shapes in the music and shapes of movement.

A flow of generational support and wisdom is a theme in Rachel's work. Fraser speaks of the uncanny revelation she had through *Edgelit*. She realized, while performing it, that the work refers to the generational continuity of women, suggesting that the young women are the older ones, and that the older women are the young ones. She describes the experience of being inside the dance as one of looking into infinity in a double mirror reflection. A challenge in *Edgelit*, she says, is to perform the work so that the whole of it is present, to call up the environment of the whole work in each moment. She has a sense of "horizon" in Rachel's work. An effect of living in big sky country for so long, perhaps, a sense of being in the kitchens of generations of prairie women, looking out the window.

Rachel is able to create an elastic sense of time. She creates gestures and movement associations which acquire meaning through being contemplated, as images in poetry often do. Her work provokes consideration.

Expert dancers crave challenges. Davida Monk finds it challenging to perform *Edgelit*, which requires a certain level of non-performance. The feet are not pointed; the body relaxes, feeling expanded through the long, long time of the solo. Skills which a dancer most often calls on in creating with a choreographer—dynamic possibilites, musicality, energy levels, textures of movement, projection—are put aside for *Edgelit*. Dancers have to seek other ways to embody the subtleties of the work. Monk considers that Rachel is sounding a new kind of performance quality through her current work, a new sensitivity to the most subtle traces of emotion and gesture in performance.

For Rachel there is a reciprocal quality, a quality of careful listening, about working with senior dancers. It is a way of refreshing approaches to creation and performance. She speaks of working with Monk to locate the utter simplicity of imagery and movement in her solo— "You stand up on the chair and you sing."

During 35th anniversary performances in December, 1998 at Winnipeg's Gas Station Theatre, Winnipeg's Contemporary Dancers presented *Edgelit*—Lisa Kuhn's solo and the quartet consisting of Davida Monk with company members Alana Shewchuk, Deborah Axelrod and Christina Medina. The work is concentrated and minimal and quite demanding for an audience.

Rachel's daughters look at this dance for four women and perceive an intimate look into a private world. They look and puzzle and question whether they are seeing themselves in *Edgelit*. But there is only the essence of feeling and gesture. Annette finds Kuhn's solo especially moving, attuned to the beauty and ugliness she sees there. She sees her mother's work as vulnerable, unsafe, with a new complexity, a different texture than earlier dances; she feels that her mother goes to the edge through her work now, instead of through performing. Rachel, as ever, is enigmatic.

⁓   ⁓   ⁓

Rachel has a reputation for giving notes to her dancers in all circumstances. After every performance, sometimes during a performance, backstage, while the dancers are ripping off one set of wet clothes and pulling on the costume for the next dance. Notes, even after the last performance of a work. But the dancers she works with expect this. It's about the work, they say, it's not unimportant. To Rachel the work is a continuum and a constant opportunity to refine, to strip away, to see a little further, to go a little deeper.

Rachel challenges the idea of dance as "finished work". This is not new for her, though the sense of one work spilling into the next is stronger now than in her earlier work. From watching Rachel's work over time, Karen Kuzak describes this long trajectory of development as characteristic. Rachel spends a long time, sometimes years, and sometimes several works exploring a theme.

Rachel loves to mix up parts of a dance, to see what the nuances might say. She enjoys reworking a dance, recasting material from one solo into another. The agony of giving birth to a new concept is over. Refining, very carefully shaping and reworking a dance with the increased objectivity allowed by the passage of time is a joyful enterprise.

Davida Monk says she has learned Rachel's hawk-like diligence, learned how to clarify, simplify and strip away what becomes non-essential in her own choreography. She has learned never to give up on the evolution of a work. Quite often there is a long process of moving away from the literal in the evolution of an artist. But there is importance in the attachment from which you are working, says Monk, as there is in a strand extended from the centre of a spider's web.

Rachel speaks with rapid-fire bursts, with hesitations and reconsiderations. She tries to think of every aspect of everything she is saying, to consider the fine detail and the design, large and small, political and personal; to discourage fuzziness. When she has cleared out all equivocation, she speaks with great clarity and authority. Pat Fraser notes this quality of speaking as symbolic of the shape of Rachel's whole artistic life. As time goes by, she cuts away all that is extraneous, honing in on what is essential and true.

Rachel continues to be sought after as a teacher. She has always, she says, had a gift for teaching. For many years she was the teacher for the dancers in her company, designing classes to help them broaden their skills and build strength. She does not teach "physiologically". To her mind, bodywork is a helpful adjunct to technical training, but one which can never replace dance class.

The cornerstones of her teaching remain ballet, Graham and Limón techniques. Ruth Currier is an original Limón company member from whom she gained a great deal of insight. Rachel found Bill Evans to be a superb teacher and through him discovered the work of kinesiologist Karen Clippinger. Rachel also cites master classes with Limón teacher Risa Steinberg and with Peggy Baker, who integrates the work of kinesiologist Irene Dowd into her teaching, as powerful influences.

Through diligent application and daily discipline, Rachel is able to remain active as a teacher. More and more, she says, she teaches her own version of what is healthful. Her strengths are in helping dancers discover what it is to be well-aligned and to help them discover simplicity and organic efficiency in motion. Her classes always include "dancey parts" in which dancers can stretch out and fly. Rachel often quotes material from her own dances, as far back as *Variations*, which she made in 1969. All these sources are a constant reminder that her art is a life's work, ongoing. "As long as I'm alive, I'm learning," she says.

Over time, Rachel reflects, she has grown more open-minded about the image of the dancer. Young, old, tall, small, full-bodied or lean, she accepts that different physical types can dance very well in different ways. This is a change from an earlier, more "autocratic" idea about who could dance well, who had good feet or a good body. It is a kind of revisioning. Earlier in her life, she danced a close and teasing duet with the ideal image of the female dancer. She tries now, she says, to be kinder as a teacher. She is more accepting of where a dancer may be at a particular time. And she says her eye is better.

Rachel surprises herself by saying things she heard from artists who made an impression on her, sometimes decades back. Suddenly, for instance, she will say, "What are you waiting for? Why not dance now?" a comment made by choreographer and teacher Dan Wagoner when he was a guest of Contemporary Dancers in the mid-1970's.

She is continually indebted to the teaching of Benjamin Harkarvy, who always stressed quality of movement. Harkarvy might explain this in a développé, saying that the dance quality of the movement, the very nature of the movement, would lessen the physical challenge. Rachel was so deeply influenced by the fineness of his musicality that to this day she may hear a piece of music and recall hearing it for the first time four decades ago in Harkarvy's ballet class. A sustaining memory of lucidity, calm and knowledge, the pursuit of one's dreams, a high and exalted addiction; a dancer's inspiration, a sense of being poised for flight, a dancer's attunement—these qualities live in Rachel. She knows what it is to be in love with dance.

Through the constant refinement of her vision, her constant watching, Rachel has arrived at a point where she trusts her intuitive responses to dancers. She is able to be extremely specific technically in rehearsal. Odette Heyn-Penner refers to her as a wonderful coach, for as well as this physical specificity, she goes after quality without quarter. There is no doubt, says Heyn-Penner, that Rachel is giving of herself too. She will not take no for an answer.

Karen Kuzak says that company dancers often say "we need Rachel." Somehow, no matter what the performance pressures are, the moment Rachel walks in to teach, everyone can relax. Dancers know that during the time they are in class with her, other cares can slip away. Rachel pays them the tribute of taking them seriously, looking at them both positively and critically. Her presence remains important in tying the Winnipeg community together with respect and dignity.

Rachel attends every dance performance in Winnipeg. Kuzak says that after performances, the dancers in her company all want to know, "Is Rachel here?" They know where she will be sitting, they wait for her. Vancouver-based choreographer Joe Laughlin, after premiering a work with the Royal Winnipeg Ballet, asked the same question. "Is Rachel here?" Her presence is essential.

Rachel, says her friend Kuzak, comes into a room like a blizzard, with her Safeway bags full of food, her cup, a teabag, the kettle set to boil. She watches the clock and takes her vitamins in a flurry. If the two choreographers happen to meet in the hallway before rehearsal, Rachel, rushing up the stairs, pauses a moment, always with the same warm greeting. "Hi, I'm so happy to see you…I'm running late for my rehearsal." And she keeps on running.

Underslept, wired on double shots of espresso, stretched thin by her wide-ranging commitments to dance and to social and political causes, Rachel remains generous with her perspective and her time. People close to her say that becoming a grandmother has mellowed her. Looking after her three young grandchildren is a very high priority for her. Rachel has been known to re-schedule and cancel commitments because of babysitting duty.

This is no light thing for her. She is making statements about women and priorities that she could not have made earlier in her life. The children's mother, Ruth, says she considers that Rachel is making up for the time she could not spend with Ruth, Miriam and Annette when they were little. She says that Rachel is very clear about what she thinks is healthy for her grandchildren. She is unstinting with her energy, playing whole-heartedly with the children, one more round of hide and go seek, one more verse of an old nursery song, even if she is exhausted.

Rachel has a close and unique rapport with each one of her daughters now. They have mirrored and transmuted some of Rachel's qualities. Each has found her own path in life, in ways which have fascinating links to their mother's interests. All of them work hard. As young women, they launched themselves into their studies. Ruth worked for a degree in kinesiology, afterward starting a studio in Winnipeg and becoming a personal trainer. Miriam worked in publicity at the Royal Winnipeg Ballet. Later she took a degree in social work and became a social worker. Annette became a nurse practicioner and university teacher. In 1999 she became the first-ever recipient of a Killam Foundation fellowship for post-graduate studies in nursing.

When Annette visits Winnipeg, she and Rachel make their journey together to Eva's grave. They stand by the stone they chose and sing a song in Yiddish, a song Eva used to sing.

Though Rachel's daughters have rued the cost of their mother's unwavering devotion to her artistic life, later in life they have made their peace with her. They speak of the challenge of having Rachel as their mother, of the cost of being close to someone so driven. Her achievements have been acute; the lessons and hardship for those closest to her have been sharp.

Rachel is valued as a mentor by many younger artists, mainly women, with whom she has worked or shared artistic aspirations. Many of her colleagues call her the "mother of contemporary dance" in Winnipeg. There is not a person connected with contemporary dance in the city who has not been touched or influenced by her in some way, as a teacher, performer, mentor, director or choreographer.

Winnipeg is a small enough city that eyebrows shot up when

choreographer Karen Kuzak proposed starting TRIP, a third contemporary dance company. She sought Rachel's counsel. "This is crazy and I understand it completely," said Rachel, "You're young, you're ambitious, you're strong. You have to build something."

Over time, Miriam Browne says, she has found that the honesty with which Rachel has faced her own struggles has given her wisdom. She is wise and calm, never vindictive in her advice to her daughter or harsh toward others. She is "a fantastic listener and an excellent support".

Many of the women she has helped, prodded, supported and believed in look to Rachel as a role model. She is a woman who does not decline or settle as she moves through life. Her horizons have not telescoped with time. All her life she has embraced change. She looks forward excitedly to the new. Stephanie Ballard tells her students that of all of them, Rachel is the most excited about the new century. Dancer Alana Shewchuk calls her an inspiration, "a living example of the possibility of life becoming more, not less".

Davida Monk speaks of how Rachel has assisted her. When she grows frustrated or tired teaching in a university environment, she looks to her friend for advice. Monk speaks of the importance of being able to put things into perspective with the help of Rachel's wisdom and experience.

Who has done this for Rachel? She has been first all along.

Faye Thomson says one of Rachel's contributions is to the evolution of the dance community itself in Canada through her involvement in its origins and in later changes. In recent years she has been knocking at the door of cultural agencies with her needs as an independent choreographer. This is thirty years after she was one of a handful who helped the shape and structure of middle-sized companies come into play on the national cultural scene.

She has helped open the window of opportunity, which has traditionally been open just a crack, and not for long, for choreographers and for people with artistic director's titles. In the face of rejection and lack of support, Rachel has asked. She has been part of the change toward more flexible circumstances for financial assistance, part of a more inclusive perspective which recognizes that options to company structures can be healthy situations for dance creation.

Seeing the maturity and changes of Rachel Browne's work poses the question of what we are missing in a larger context. Rachel's tenacity is unique. How many artists are there, with what astonishing visions and wisdom to offer, who can not find the means to make their art, or who decide to walk a less arduous path? Rachel dislikes the word pioneer, feeling that it throws light on the past more than toward the future. She is uncomfortable with the suggestion that she is exceptional. She insists on the validity of change, and on ensuring that her voice is heard.

To say, as Rachel does, that women do not have to disappear in middle age is radical. To say that womens' inner lives are important, precious, poetic, expressible, is extreme. To say that a dance career can continue to evolve as one grows older is genderlessly bold, and a mark of great courage in a woman. To say that a dance creator's work can evolve with integrity outside the flow of fashion is unusually important.

These are not points Rachel sets out deliberately to make. She is doing her work. For Rachel, the end of this extraordinary trailbreaking has been to bring her closer to her own voice, to liberate the creative being who for so long gave away her song. Rachel is clear and present, committed to the work of dance.

The link between physical and expressive fullness is always fascinating. Often the most skilled dancers create choreographic work which is brilliant, dancerly and physically challenging. As they move away from connection to the immediacy of the dancer's body they often change perspective.

The eye changes as the I changes. Sometimes a larger potential emerges, a bigger view of stage, or of dramatic possibilities. A more objective creative point of view comes with maturity—cooler perhaps, not so heated by direct physical urgency, by the ardent act of dancing. Women who have persevered as far as Rachel has into their choreographic careers are few and far between, although it was true of Agnes de Mille and Martha Graham. As they extricated themselves from stage personae, they found other sources to mine. For Graham it was the mythic, the folkloric, the virtues and challenges of pioneer America, to which she felt enduringly and personally connected. She invented a New World way of moving, integral to a fresh view of the world in a burgeoning century. Grown in America, not European in origin.

Many of Rachel's earlier dances melded her politics and her art. In a way they looked back to an earlier time. For many significant figures of American modern dance, José Limón, Jane Dudley, Paul Taylor, among many others, art was a way of speaking about the world. Works of a whole era of American modern dance were tied to idealism and political aims. Certain of Rachel's politically-themed works, *In A Dark Time the Eye Begins to See*, *To the Year 2000* and others, were made in this spirit. Alana Shewchuk calls these Rachel's "war dances". Rachel calls them "peace" or "hope" dances. They reflect her lifelong concern with working for global peace and justice.

Over time her politics and feminism have aligned. She continues to be involved and concerned with environmental and political issues. But the focus of her work is closer to home, closer to the bone, pared away to a song of women.

Rachel's subject is women, her expression of her feeling about women and women's expressions of who they are and who they want to be. She looks at her own long path of motherhood, of her daughterhood, of her early years with her own daughters, of her mother's dying and of the joy she takes in her grandchildren. She is interested in the whole range of the voices of women, in radical feminism, in lesbianism—in all of women's expression.

Over the long bridge of her time and life experience Rachel has arrived at this certainty of her voice, her subject and the ground of all her work to come. Fundamental to her dance is a sense of rhythm and tension. She can do whatever she chooses now.

Ann Southam has been intrigued by the qualities of Rachel's choreography and suggested further creative collaboration with Rachel. In the spring of 1999 Rachel began work on what is projected to be a new series of solos called "Older Women Dance". Southam asked Rachel to make a dance for Susan Macpherson, "whose very being," says the composer, "is a dance." In the early summer of 1999 Rachel started working in Winnipeg with Stephanie Ballard and Odette Heyn-Penner on other parts of this project. "It is second nature for both Odette and me to be fully engaged in the process and extend a supporting arm to the elder we so love and admire," says Ballard. "The experience is inspired and motivating."

Although Southam, an eminent composer, has worked with many choreographers, among them Patricia Beatty, David Earle, Peter Randazzo, Christopher House, Peggy Baker and Anna Blewchamp, the work with Rachel is ongoing and a point of mutual exchange. Southam's captivation by silence finds a physical counterpart in Rachel's fascination with resonant stillness.

"I love it," Southam says of Rachel's dances, "when the dancers stop moving. Just stop. It's such an amazing thing to do, for anybody to do. Stop moving."

In the pursuit of essence and simplicity, the two artists have arrived at a similar point in different disciplines. They both explain this as a search for something. Southam says of her search for clarity, "I don't care how long it takes, or how boring it is, I've got to do it, otherwise I'll go nuts. You can listen if you want, I don't care! For a long time I think I was trying to be somebody musically that I wasn't. Now…you just have to do what you have to do, and find what you're looking for. There just isn't the time for pretending and trying to be interesting for the sake of being interesting."

Rachel echoes this conviction. Anyone, she says, who has spent a lifetime as a creative artist and has her two feet on the earth will speak like this. To have reached a certain point in life and still be working in the arts is a statement of commitment without pretense, echoing a strong sense of self and reality.

Rachel's most recent dances seem to come from a place where dance and music are one, where listening is speaking, where the present looks to the past and future; a place of vibrant stillness.

Rachel Browne, brave soloist, dogged perfectionist, the woman who will not give up. Rachel has known trouble in her life. Honesty, gutsiness and vigilance have won her wisdom. Although she is not an old woman, she enlivens the third age of women, walking before friends who will follow her, calling back. Her story twines with the myths and stories which growl beneath her present work. There is something of everywoman in Rachel Browne, and something of the heroine's still-uncharted journey. She is a first mover, courageous, elemental, drawn on by intense artistic curiosity.

Odette Heyn-Penner tells a favourite story about Rachel to her students. Rachel has always loved the sun. Sometimes she leaves Contemporary Dancers' studios to walk up and down Pulford Street outside the Augustine Church, looking for the warmth of the sun. And she always finds it. Painting an image of inspiration in motion, Heyn-Penner describes how Rachel raises her chest and her face to the sun and stands, drinking at the source of what she finds constant and true. Heat, light, purity, essential forces.

Then, being Rachel, she plunges back inside—into her moving world, this work of dance that she loves.

Dance Works by Rachel Browne
A Chronology

1954 *Mozart's Country Dances*
Group work created in New York withthe New Century Dancers
Premiere: Jewish Educational Alliance Theater, New York City

1962 *Brahms' Waltzes*
Group work created for the Lhotka Ballet Studio

1963 *Girl with the Flaxen Hair*
Music: Claude Debussy
Solo: Marilyn Lewis, student at the Lhotka Ballet Studio

1964 *Odetta's Songs and Dances*
Music: Odetta
Group work for Contemporary Dancers
Premiere: University of Manitoba, Winnipeg
Shared program with Marta Hidy Trio
Contemporary Dancers' inaugural performance

1964 *Turmoil*
Music: Bela Bartók
Group work
Premiere: University of Manitoba, Winnipeg
Shared program with Marta Hidy Trio
Contemporary Dancers' inaugural performance

1965 *Take Five*
Music: Dave Brubeck
Group work
Premiere: Winnipeg

1965 *Appalachian Spring*
Music: Aaron Copland, "Appalachian Spring"
Group work
Premiere: Winnipeg

1966 *Evening in the Suburbs*
Music: original score Victor Davies
Poetry by Raymond Souster
Sextet (6 women)
Premiere: Winnipeg

1967 *Three Faces of Jazz*
Music: Don Shirley
Group dance
Premiere: Winnipeg

1967 *Anerca* (remounted 1972)
Music: Edgar Varese, Tzvi Avni, Walter Carlos
Inuit chants, read by Renee Jamieson
Group work for Contemporary Dancers
Premiere: Winnipeg

1967 *Pas le Même Pas*
Music: Gary Gross
Quintet (five women)
Premiere: Winnipeg, spring season 1967

1967 *The Urge*
Music: unknown
Trio for women
Premiere: Winnipeg

1968 *Where the Shining Trumpets Blow*
(remounted in 1973 as a 40-minute group work)
Music: Gustav Mahler, "Das Knaben Wunderhorn"
Trio for women
Premiere: Playhouse Theatre, Winnipeg

1968 *Miles Smiles*
Music: Miles Davis
Sextet
Premiere: April 26, Manitoba Theatre Centre, Winnipeg

1968 *New Songs and Dances*
Music: Odetta
Group work
Premiere: April 26, Manitoba Theatre Centre, Winnipeg

1968 *Contrasts (I)*
Music: Béla Bartók
Group work
Premiere: Winnipeg

1969 *Cante Hondo*
Music: Ohana
Group work
Premiere: Feb. 28, Playhouse Theatre, Winnipeg

1969 *Variations*
Music: J.S. Bach, "The Goldberg Variations"
Group work
Premiere: Playhouse Theatre, Winnipeg

1969 *Theme and Rock*
Music: Bob McMullin
Group dance
Premiere: performed with the Winnipeg Symphony Orchestra and The Guess Who, Winnipeg

1971 *Rhythming*
Music: original drum solo score by Billy Graham
Solo
Premiere: St. Mary's Academy, Winnipeg

1972 *Blues & Highs*
Music: Laura Nyro
Group work
Premiere: Playhouse Theatre, Winnipeg

1974 *Contrasts (II)*
Music: Béla Bartók
Group dance
Premiere: Playhouse Theatre, Winnipeg

1975 *Cameo*
Music: J.S. Bach
Solo
premiere: Playhouse Theatre, Winnipeg

1975 *The Woman I Am*
Music: original score by Paul Horn
Poetry by Dorothy Livesay and Miriam Mandel, read by Renee Jamieson
Group work
Premiere: Playhouse Theatre, Winnipeg

1976 *Interiors*
Music: Jim Donahue; lyrics after Dorothy Livesay
Duet: Rachel Browne and Ken Lipitz
Premiere: Playhouse Theatre, Winnipeg

1976 *In Praise*
Music: J.S. Bach (played by harpsichordist Wanda Landowska)
Group work
Premiere: Playhouse Theatre, Winnipeg

1976 *Five Cameos*
Music: J.S. Bach
Group work
Premiere: Playhouse Theatre, Winnipeg

1976 *Continuum (I)*
Music: Johannes Brahms
Duet: Rachel Browne and Stephanie Ballard
Premiere: Playhouse Theatre, Winnipeg

1977 *Just About Us*
Music: original score by Jim Donahue
Duet: Rachel Browne and Suzanne Oliver
Premiere: Playhouse Theatre, Winnipeg

1978 *The Other*
Music: Maurice Ravel
Poetry by Dorothy Livesay and Adrienne Rich
Duet: Rachel Browne and Ken Lipitz
Premiere: Playhouse Theatre, Winnipeg

1978 *Birthday Offering*
Music: W.A. Mozart
Solo: Roger Smith
Premiere: Playhouse Theatre, Winnipeg

1979 *Solitude*
Music: Johannes Brahms
Group work
Premiere: Playhouse Theatre, Winnipeg

1980 *To the Year 2000*
Music: Bela Bartók
Titled after a poem by Pablo Neruda
Trio
Premiere: January 24, Playhouse Theatre, Winnipeg

1980 *untitled*
Music: J.S. Bach
Solo: Alana Shewchuk, dedicated to Benjamin Harkarvy
Premiere: Playhouse Theatre, Winnipeg

1981 *Dreams*
Text from dancers' dreams
Trio
After a sketch made at the National Choreographic Seminar, Banff Centre for the
Arts, 1980
Premiere: Playhouse Theatre, Winnipeg

1981 *Haiku*
Music: original score by Owen Clarke
Duet: Rachel Browne and Ruth Cansfield
Premiere: Manitoba Theatre Centre, Winnipeg

1982 *M.L.W.*
Music: Mary Lou Williams
Solo and trio
Premiere: Warehouse Theatre, Manitoba Theatre Centre, Winnipeg

1982 *Revival*
Music: original score by Jim Donahue based on original songs
Group dance
Premiere: Playhouse Theatre, Winnipeg

1983 *Shalom*
Music: J.S. Bach
Solo: Rachel Browne
Premiere: Brigantine Room, Harbourfront Centre, Toronto

1984 *A Jest of God*
Music: original score by Jim Donahue
Text from *A Jest of God* by Margaret Laurence
Group work
Premiere: Gas Station Theatre, Winnipeg

1985 *Camping Out*
(Choreography and concept by Tedd Robinson, with choreographic contributions by
Murray Darroch and Rachel Browne)
music: Franz Liszt
Solo: Desiree Kleeman
Premiere: Gas Station Theatre, Winnipeg

1985 *To the New Year*
Music: Diana McIntosh
Text: Denise Levertov and Muriel Rukeyser
Premiere: Winnipeg, Contemporary Dancers' 20th anniversary celebrations, March,
1985

★★★ All works preceding were created for Contemporary Dancers except where indicated. Rachel
Browne's independent works begin next.

1985 *The Cry*
Music: Bernard Xolotol
Text: Denise Levertov
Trio: Jeanette Angel, Karen Kuzak and Bruce Mitchell
Premiere: Professional Program of WCD School, WCD Studios, Winnipeg

1987 *Old Times Now*
Music: Almeta Speaks
Solo: D-Anne Kuby
Premiere: program of Rachel Browne's work, June 19, 1987, Gas Station Theatre, Winnipeg

1987 solo for Christopher Gower
Performed as part of an evening of work titled *Shalom*, with Rachel Browne performing her solo "Shalom", and Alana Shewchuk performing the untitled 1980 Bach solo premiere: Gas Station Theatre, Winnipeg

1987 *In a Dark Time the Eye Begins to See*
Music: Johann Pachelbel, Vangelis
Text: Robert Jay Lifton
Originally created at York University for a large ensemble; premiered at Premiere Dance Theatre, Toronto, in 1987; later remounted for an ensemble of eight dancers
Premiere: Rachel Browne, A Retrospective, June 8, 1989, Gas Station Theatre, Winnipeg

1988 *Ballade*
Music: Frédéric Chopin
Group work/remounted in 1989 for Professional Program of WCD School
Premiere: Burton Auditorium, York University, Toronto

1988 *Tres Bailes Enigmaticos*
Music: three Spanish songs, performed by Montserrat Caballé and Alice Artzt
Premiere: Women and the Arts Festival, Winnipeg

1989 *Sunset Sentences*
Music: Samuel Barber, Diana McIntosh
Quintet (five women)
Premiere: May 1989, Festival of Canadian Modern Dance, Gas Station Theatre, Winnipeg

1990 *Fine, Thank You!*
Music: Odetta singing the blues
Three solos and one duet
Premiere: May 1990, Festival of Canadian Modern Dance, Gas Station Theatre, Winnipeg

1990 *My Romance*
Music: Rogers & Hart, Hoagy Carmichael, arranged and performed by Almeta Speaks
Solo: Sharon Moore
Premiere: September 14, 1990, Gas Station Theatre, Winnipeg

1990 *Continuum (II)*
Music: J.S. Bach
Duet: Rachel Browne and Odette Heyn-Penner
Premiere: September 14, 1990, Gas Station Theatre, Winnipeg

1990 *Cuba Libra*
Music: Leo Brouwer
Solo: Sharon Moore
Premiere: September 14, 1990, Gas Station Theatre, Winnipeg

1990 *Shout*
Music: Aretha Franklin
Solo: Constance Cooke
Premiere: September 14, 1990, Gas Station Theatre, Winnipeg

1991 *Freddy*
Music: Kurt Weill, sung by Teresa Stratas
Solo: Sharon Moore
Premiere: July 17, 1991, Winnipeg Fringe Festival
Manitoba Theatre Centre's Warehouse Theatre, Winnipeg

1991 *Pat's Bach*
Music: J.S. Bach, "Partita #5 in G Major", played by Glenn Gould
Solo: Patricia Fraser
Premiere: August 9, 1991, fringe Festival of Independent Dance Artists (fFIDA) Winchester Street Theatre, Toronto

1991 *Images*
Music: Debussy
Trio (3 women)
Premiere: September 13, 1991, Gas Station Theatre, Winnipeg

1991 *For David*
Music: Traditional Sephardic songs
Solo: Brent Lott
Created in memory of David Tucker
Premiere: September 13, 1991, Gas Station Theatre, Winnipeg

1991 *If Not Now*
Music: Tracy Chapman
Solo: Julia Zohrab
Premiere: July 17, 1991, Winnipeg Fringe Festival, Manitoba Theatre Centre, Winnipeg

1992 *Dreamrite*
Music: Diana McIntosh (original score)
Quintet (five women)
Premiere: INDE Festival, duMaurier Theatre, Toronto

1992 *Sharonblue*
Music: Cole Porter
Solo: Sharon Moore
Premiere: August 14, 1992, fFIDA, Winchester Street Theatre, Toronto

1992 *Mouvement*
Music: Bernard Xolotol
Solo: Alana Shewchuk
Premiere: September 11, 1992, program of Rachel Browne's work, Gas Station Theatre, Winnipeg

1993 *Four Haiku*
Music: Bernard Xolotol
Four intersecting solos for women
Premiere: October 22, 1993, program of Rachel Browne's work, Gas Station Theatre, Winnipeg

1994 *K.J.3*
Music: Keith Jarrett
Trio; created for the Canadian Children's Dance Theatre; later remounted in Winnipeg for the Professional Program, WCD School, as *K.J.4*
Premiere: duMaurier Theatre, Toronto

1995 *Toward Light*
Music: J.S. Bach, Ann Southam
Cast of eleven women
Premiere: Gas Station Theatre, Winnipeg

1995 *Re-tuning, or The Great Canadian Hoedown*
Music: Ann Southam, "Re-tuning"
Originally created for twelve dancers at the Canadian Children's Dance Theatre; remounted, 1995, for an ensemble of ten dancers, Professional Program, WCD School
Premiere: WCD Studios, Winnipeg

1996 *Six Messages*
Music: Ann Southam, "Music for Slow Dancing"
Created for the Professional Program of WCD School
Premiere: Gas Station Theatre, Winnipeg

1996 *Edgelit*
music: Ann Southam, "Music for Slow Dancing"
solo created for Davida Monk
Premiere: Calgary

1997 *Willow Island*
Music: The Penguin Café Orchestra
Created for the Professional Program, WCD School
Premiere: Gas Station Theatre, Winnipeg

1997 *Four Messages*
Music: Ann Southam, "Music for Slow Dancing"
Quartet
Premiere: Dancers' Studio West, Calgary

1998 *Edgelit*
Music: Ann Southam, "Soundstill"
Solo: Lisa Kuhn
Premiere: Regina

1998 *Edgelit*
Music: Ann Southam, "Fluke Sound", "Soundstill", "Music for Slow Dancing"
New solo for Pat Fraser, solo for Lisa Kuhn, quartet for Davida Monk and three
younger dancers
Premiere: June, 1998, WCD studios, Winnipeg

1999 *Remembering Summer*
Music: Ann Southam, "Slow Dances"
New solo for Susan Macpherson
Part of "Older Women Dance" project, an extension of *Edgelit*
To be performed with revised *Edgelit* solo for Davida Monk with the trio of Stephanie
Ballard, Rachel Browne and Odette Heyn-Penner
Music: Ann Southam, "Music for Slow Dancing"
Premiere: November 4, 1999, Centre culturel franco-manitobain, Winnipeg

SOURCES

Publications and Reviews

Anderson, Carol. 1998. Rachel Browne. *The International Dictionary of Modern Dance*, St. James Press, Detroit, Michigan.

Anderson, Jack. "Dancing in a January World: Winnipeg's Contemporary Dancers," *Dance Magazine*, March, 1977.

Brownell, Kathryn. "Toronto Dance Festival," *Dance in Canada* 19 (Spring, 1979): 19-20.

Buchholz, Garth. "Cameos poignant, breathtaking," *Winnipeg Free Press*, Saturday, October 24, 1993.

Citron, Paula. "Women pour out hearts at DanceWorks festival," *Toronto Star*, Sunday, April 18, 1993.

Citron, Paula. "Radio Review of Rachel Browne's *Four Haiku*," August, 1993, fFIDA Festival, Toronto.

Crabb, Michael. "Contemporary Dancers Offers Head-Spinning Mix," *Dance Magazine*, August, 1985.

Crabb, Michael. "Fringe Festival of Independent Dance Artists," *Dance Connection*, November/December/January 1993-94.

de Mille, Agnes. 1960. *To A Young Dancer: A Handbook*, Little, Brown and Company, New York.

Dafoe, Christopher. 1990. *Dancing Through Time: The First Fifty Years of Canada's Royal Winnipeg Ballet*, Portage & Main Press, Winnipeg, Manitoba.

Enright, Robert. "Rachel Browne, A Retrospective," *The Arts Tonight*, CBC Radio, June 9, 1989.

Enright, Robert. "Contemporary Dancers: A Prairie Lament becomes a Song of Hope." *Dance in Canada* 34 (Winter, 1982):20-23.

Forzley, Richard. "Contemporary Dancers Canada: New Directions," *Dance in Canada* 44 (Summer, 1985): 4-9.

Forzley, Richard. "Telling the Dancer from the Dance," *Border Crossings*, Fall, 1985.

Gildner, Alina. "Evening belongs to Torontonian," *The Globe and Mail*, April 17, 1993.

Gildner, Alina. "Jabberwocky of movement holds up a looking-glass," *The Globe and Mail*, Saturday, August 10, 1991.

Good, Jacqui. "Rachel Browne." from the *Dictionary of Theatrical Dance*, Dance Collection Danse Press/es, Toronto, 1997.

Good, Jacqui. "Winnipeg: Rachel Browne, The Dance Collective, Contemporary Dancers, Royal Winnipeg Ballet—Fall 1992," *Dance Connection*, February/March, 1993.

Good, Jacqui. "Dance-Maker: The Turbulent and Moving Times of Rachel Browne." *Border Crossings,* Fall, 1989, 59-63.

Good, Jacqui. "An Evening with Rachel Browne," CBC Review, Saturday, June 20, 1987.

Good, Jacqui. "Contemporary Dancers," *Dance in Canada* 38 (Winter, 1983-84): 37.

Jowitt, Deborah. "Dance," *The Village Voice*, September 26, 1977.

McCracken, Melinda. "A 30th Anniversary in Winnipeg," Dance Collection Danse *The News* 36 (1994): 4-7.

McDonagh, Don. "Jacob's Pillow," *The New York Times*, August 25, 1977.

McDonagh, Don. 1970. *The Rise and Fall and Rise of Modern Dance*, Mentor Books, The New American Library, New York.

Morriss, Frank. "Show Beat," *Winnipeg Free Press*, March 3, 1969.

Noticeboard, *Dance in Canada* 14 (Fall/Winter, 1977-78): 38.

Olver, Michael. "Dancing Group Develops Public," *Winnipeg Tribune*, April 7, 1966.

O'Toole, Lawrence. "Troupe fuses varying styles into perfect blend," *The Globe and Mail*, Toronto, February 11, 1976.

O'Reilly, Finnbar. "Three exquisite pieces of dance choreography," *The Globe and Mail*, Toronto, August 21, 1998.

Percival, John. 1970. *Modern Ballet*, Studio Vista/Dutton, London, England, 78-81.

Rabin, Linda. 1998. "Remembering The White Goddess" from *This Passion: for the love of dance*, edited by Carol Anderson, Dance Collection Danse Press/es, Toronto, 51-69.

Review of *Anerca*. *Dance in Canada* 4 (Spring, 1975): 14-17.

Singen, Kevin. "Contemporary Dancers," *Dance in Canada* 16 (Summer, 1978): 27-28.

Stringer, Muriel. "Contemporary Dancers." *Dance in Canada* 31 (Spring, 1982): 33-34.

Windreich, Leland. 1998. "Tudor's Psyche." *Dance Encounters—Leland Windreich Writing on Dance*, Dance Collection Danse Press/es, Toronto, 192-199.

Wyman, Max. 1978. *The Royal Winnipeg Ballet: The First Forty Years*, Doubleday Canada Limited, Toronto.

Other Reviews

Kostelnuk, Michael. "Contemporary Dancers: An Interesting Show," Winnipeg, May 13, 1967.

"Dancers Triumph at Expo," *The Winnipeg Tribune's Weekend Showcase*, Saturday, July 29, 1967.

INTERVIEWS AND ACKNOWLEDGMENTS

Carol Anderson's conversation with Rachel Browne is ongoing—including interviews in March 1995, July 1995, November 1996, May 1998, July 1998, December 1998, and April and May 1999 in Toronto, Ottawa and Winnipeg.

Conversations with relatives, colleagues and friends of Rachel Browne have been a main source for writing about Rachel and her work. Many thanks to all for their openness and generosity.

Thank you to
Ruth Asper, Winnipeg
Stephanie Ballard, Winnipeg
Annette Browne, Prince George, B.C.
Miriam Browne, Winnipeg
Ruth Cansfield, Winnipeg
Patricia Fraser, Toronto
Odette Heyn-Penner, Winnipeg
Karen Kuzak, Winnipeg
Deborah Lundmark, Toronto
Davida Monk, Calgary
Sharon Moore, Toronto
Gaile Petursson-Hiley, Winnipeg
Tedd Senmon Robinson, Ottawa
Richard Rutherford, Ottawa
Alana Shewchuk, Winnipeg
Ben Sokoloff, Toronto
Ann Southam, Toronto
Grant Strate, Vancouver
Tom Stroud, Winnipeg
Faye Thomson, Winnipeg

Carol Anderson also consulted Melinda McCracken's interviews with Rachel Browne, which took place in Winnipeg in June, 1994.

Videotapes and a catalogued list of Rachel Browne's choreography (compiled by Rachel Browne) from 1963-1994 were consulted at Dance Collection Danse, Toronto.

THANKS

Stephanie Ballard's Legacy Project repertory and performance lists for Contemporary Dancers were invaluable references for the company's history.

Special thanks to Stephanie Ballard, for so generously sharing her memories and her Legacy Project work. Thank you to Alanna Keefe, for finding ways to bring this writing to light. Thank you to Rachel, for believing in this book. Thanks to Marilyn Biderman for reading and commenting on the manuscript. Thank you to Lawrence and Miriam Adams for vision and generous encouragement.

Thank you to Michael Vaughan, for all the editorial input and for gifts of time. Thank you for supporting my writing habit.

INDEX

A
A Jest of God, 102, 104, 151
Alexandrowicz, Conrad, 80-81
Alis, Jill, 61
Alonso, Alicia, 26
Anerca, 61, 62, 68, 75, 115, 148
Appalachian Spring, 147
Aragon Ballroom. *See* Contemporary Dancers, locations
Ashton, Gwynne, 44
Asper, Ruth, 71
Augustine Church. *See* Contemporary Dancers, locations
Axelrod, Deborah, 137

B
Balanchine, George, 26
Ballade, 152
Ballard, Stephanie, 54, 69, 70, 71, 72, 80-81, 92
    conflict with, 93-96,105, 115, 142, 145
Banff Choreographic Seminar, 92, 93
Darsky, Barbara, 61
Bartók, Béla, 53, 74
Belkin, Cheryl, 61
Birthday Offering, 150
Blewchamp, Anna, 80, 81, 83, 145
Blues & Highs, 149
Bolender, Todd, 32, 92
Boris, Ruthanna, 37, 39, 50
Botkin, Nancy, 112
Brahms' Waltzes, 147
Browne, Annette (daughter), 53, 57-58, 88, 90, 91, 97, 126, 137, 141
Browne, Don (first husband). *See* Browne, Rachel, and Don Browne
Browne, Miriam (daughter), 57-58, 66, 71, 97, 128, 131, 134, 141, 142
Browne, Rachel
    and Ben Sokolof (second husband) and, 88, 96, 130, 134
    and Don Browne (first husband) and, 27-31, 47, 56
        appetite of, 24-25, 28-29, 83
        awards of, 59, 83, 109, 129, 131
        children, 47-50, 53. *See also* Browne, Annette; Browne, Miriam; Browne, Ruth
        discipline, 49, 83, 128, 131

early years, 15-18
    fear of fire, 30
    feminism, 87, 107, 134, 140, 144
    inspiration from nature, 120, 132, 146
    inspiration to others, 122-28, 132, 132, 139, 141-42
    method. *See* Browne, Rachel, philosophy
    mid-life, 88-90, 91, 108-9, 118, 131
    modern dance views, 26-28, 43, 51-56, 65
    motherhood, 47-50
    music, 33
    Oklahoma!, 31-32
    parents, 15, 16, 17-18, 19-20, 29, 31, 45, 50-51, 57, 109, 121-22
    philosophy, 55-56, 87-88, 91, 126-28, 135-45
    physique, 20, 34-35, 42-43
    politics, 18-19, 27, 28, 30, 131, 134, 138, 144
    role model, 141-43
    teaching, 138-39. *See also* Browne, Rachel, career periods of
    tenacity, 20-21, 22, 25-26, 33-34, 35, 36, 40, 45, 49, 93, 96-99, 102, 143
Browne, Rachel, ballet and
    growing away from ballet, 51
    love of ballet, 20-21, 26, 27, 31-32, 38, 45, 47, 48, 138
Browne, Rachel, career periods
    Lhotka Ballet Studio, 50-52, 56, 57, 65, 71, 114, 130, 138-40
    New York (city), 15, 24-35
    Philadelphia, 15-20
    Royal Winnipeg Ballet, 35-46
    University of Calgary, 130
    York University (Toronto), 107-8
Browne, Rachel, choreography, 27, 31, 34, 37, 43, 55, 61, 69, 75, 79, 80, 91, 104-7, 143-45. *See also* Browne, Rachel, dances
Browne, Rachel, creative phases, 79, 91-93, 104
    Four Haiku (1993), 122-24
    Mouvement (1992), 116-17, 120-24
Browne, Rachel, dances, 31-32
    choreographed, 28, 51-54, 61, 71, 74, 85, 86, 105-9, 115-37, 133, 135
    performed, 38-39, 40, 41, 42, 43, 44, 53, 60-70, 74-75, 80-86, 89, 90-93, 108, 119, 133
Browne, Richard, 62
Browne, Ruth (daughter), 86, 121, 131, 134, 141

Bruhn, Erik, 26
Burton, Irving, 27
Butler, John, 32

C
Cameo, 81, 84, 149
Camping Out, 151
Canada Council for the Arts, 37, 53, 54, 59-60, 61, 78, 91, 94-95, 105, 109, 112
Canadian Children's Dance Theatre, 64, 120
Cansfield, Ruth, 80-81, 90, 93, 96, 98, 105, 106
Cante Hondo, 149
Caton, Edward, 23, 25
Clouser, James, 40, 62, 75
Cohen, Ze'eva, 80
Contemporary Dancers (Winnipeg) dance company, 43, 45, 53-105, 107, 110-17, 131
    barring Rachel Browne's entry, 111-12
    Browne's choreography workshops, 80
    Browne's report to *Winnipeg Free Press*, 112
    Browne's work without pay, 114
    choreography by Browne. *See* Browne, Rachel, dances
    choreography by others, 61-63, 70, 73-75, 79-88, 92, 103-104, 115
    conflicts of vision. *See* Ballard, Stephanie; Moulton, Charlie; Holloway, Bob; Polish, Evelyn; Muller, Rick; Scurfield, Tom
    dismissal of Browne, 95-101
    financial problems, 91, 95, 113-14
    locations, 68, 78, 80, 146
    name change, 103
    performances, 61-63, 70, 71, 73-75, 79-88, 92, 103-9, 115-19, 120, 121-37, 144
    post-1991 conditions, 113
    reinstatement of Browne, 113
    US tours, 81-84. *See also* School of Contemporary Dancers
Continuum, 121, 124, 150, 153
Contrasts, 74, 115, 148, 149
Cooke, Constance, 118
Cry, The, 152
Cuba Libra, 153
Cunningham, Merce, 27, 54, 110
Currier, Ruth, 54

D
D'Amboise, Jacque, 26
Dance Collective, 98
Dance Discovery, 92
Davies, Victor, 61
Davis, James, 80
de Mille, Agnes, 21, 26, 31, 48, 143
Delta Drum Dancers, 68
Donahue, Jim, 85, 86
Double residencies. *See* Stroud, Tom
Dowd, Irene, 139
Dreamrite, 117, 121, 154
Dreams, 151
Duncan, Miss, 19
Dyck, Agnetha, 125

E
Earle, David, 80, 82, 83, 145
Edgelit, 109, 117, 119, 129, 130, 134, 135, 136, 137, 154, 155
Evans, Bill, 99, 102, 103, 138
Evening in the Suburbs, 61, 148

F
Farally, Betty, 44-45
Father Divine, 24
Festival of Canadian Modern Dance, 103
Fine, Thank You!, 111, 152
Five Cameos, 80, 150
Flanders, Charles, 80
Fontaine, Janice, 78
For David, 124, 153
Four Haiku, 117, 119, 122, 124, 154
Four Messages, 130, 155
Frankel, Emily, 32
Fraser, Patricia, 107-8, 122, 123, 126, 134, 135
Freddy, 118, 119, 153

G
Gain, Richard, 74
Gamson, Annabelle, 83
Gendel, Harriet, 27, 29, 30, 31
Girl with the Flaxen Hair, 147
Goldstein, Rosalie, 77, 85
Goodwin, Betty, 120
    artistic parallel with Rachel Browne, 120
Graham technique, 54. *See also* Graham, Martha
Graham, Martha, 26, 27, 32, 54, 72, 138, 143
Greenberg, Eva (mother). *See* Minkoff, Eva
Griffin, Rodney, 80, 84

H
Haiku, 90, 103, 106, 151
Harkarvy, Benjamin, 23, 25, 27, 29, 32-35, 39, 42, 44, 139
    resignation from RWB, 39
    Royal Winnipeg Ballet, 34, 37-39
Hayden, Melissa, 26, 32, 34
Heyn-Penner, Odette, 72, 89, 113, 114, 115, 126, 130, 132, 133, 140, 145, 146
Hinkson, Mary, 32
Hirsch, John, 44
Hobi, Frank, 37
Holahan, William, 74
Holloway, Bob, 59, 67-68, 71, 73, 76
    conflict with, 76-77
Horn & Hardart Automat, 25-26, 28
Horn, Paul, 85
Hunter, Terry, 102

I
If Not Now, 153
Images, 153
In a Dark Time the Eye Begins to See, 106-7, 121, 144, 152
In Praise, 150
Ingram, Jennifer, 61

Interiors, 80, 81, 83, 85, 86, 81, 149
Irish, Richard, 112

J
Jamieson, Karen, 79, 102, 113
Jarrett, Keith, 120
Joffrey, Robert, 25, 32, 33
Johnson, Karen, 113
Judson Church movement, 69
Juliard School, 33
Just About Us, 82, 83, 86, 108, 150

K
K.J.3, 119, 120, 130, 154
Keefe, Alanna, 113
Keenberg, Ron, 104
Kent, Allegra, 26, 32, 34
Keuter, Cliff, 80, 83, 103
Korol, Taras, 68
Kuby, D-Anne, 93, 96, 106, 107, 111
Kuhn, Lisa, 119, 135, 136, 137
Kuzak, Karen, 82, 89, 111, 117, 125, 126, 127, 137, 140, 142

L
Lander, Judith, 84, 89
Lewis, Lillian, 44
Lewis, Marilyn, 61
Lhotka, Nenad, 50, 52, 54, 62
Limón technique, 54, 81
Limón, José, 27, 54, 138, 144
Lipitz, Kenneth, 80, 81, 85, 86
Littlefield Ballet School (Philadelphia), 21
Livesay, Dorothy, 84, 85, 86, 87
Lloyd, Gweneth, 37, 39, 44
Lundmark, Deborah, 63-64, 120

M
M.L.W., 93, 151
Macdonald, Brian, 39-40, 44
Macpherson, Susan, 144
Macquire, Terrill, 117
Mahler, Elfrieda, 19, 24
Mandel, Miriam, 85
Manitoba Arts Council, 104, 105, 109, 112, 135
Marcuse, Judith, 79, 83, 84
Mascall, Jennifer, 79
Maslow, Sophie, 32, 70, 84
Matthews, Fred, 81
Mazzo, Kay, 26
McBride, Patricia, 26
McCarthy era, 27
McDonagh, Don, 81
McIntosh, Diana, 117
Medina, Christina, 137
Miles Smiles, 62, 148
Minkoff, Eva (mother). *See* Browne, Rachel, parents
Minkoff, Israel (father). *See* Browne, Rachel, parents
Minkoff, Ray, 15

Monk, Davida, 117, 119, 122, 125, 126, 127, 130, 135, 136, 137, 142
Moore, Sharon, 118, 119, 122, 126, 127
Morrice, Norman, 80, 83
Moulton, Charlie, 43
    conflict with, 110-13
Moulton, Robert, 43, 51, 62, 69, 74, 110
Mouvement, 115, 116-19, 120, 121, 124, 154
Mozart's Country Dances, 147
Muller, Rick, 90
    conflict and, 90, 94-96
My Romance, 119, 124, 130, 153

N
Nann, Andrea, 107, 119
National Ballet of Canada, 37
Nenad and Jill Lhotka Ballet Studio (Winnipeg), 50
New Century Dancers, 27, 28
New Songs and Dances, 148
New York Dance Drama Company, 32
Newman, Rosalind, 27
Nikolais, Alwin, 24
Noonan, Nancy, 41

O
Oberlander, Ellen, 112
Odetta's Songs and Dances, 53, 54, 57, 61, 62, 87, 106, 115, 147
Old Times Now, 106-7, 119, 152
Older Women Dance, 144
Oliver, Susan, 86, 108
Ormandy, Eugene, 22
Other, The, 103, 150

P
Paris, Nancy, 80
Pas le Même Pas, 61, 62, 148
Pat's Bach, 108, 118, 119, 153
Permit, Naomi, 78
Perreault, Jean-Pierre, 92, 113, 114
Petursson-Hiley, Gaile, 80, 82, 89, 92, 93, 96, 98, 105
Polish, Evelyn, 91, 92, 95
Psychological ballets. *See* Tudor, Anthony

R
Rabin, Linda 79
Ravitz, Paula, 79
Re-tuning, or the Great Canadian Hoedown, 120, 154
Red Hook, 31
Remembering Summer, 155
Revival, 151
Rhythming, 149
Rich, Adrienne, 87
Richardson, Kathleen, 36
Robbins, Jerome, 26
Robinson, Tedd, 80-81, 83, 93, 102-3, 104, 111, 115
Rondo ad Absurdum, 74

Royal Winnipeg Ballet, 33, 34, 37, 38, 39, 40, 48, 50, 74, 82, 88
Rune to a Green Star, 70, 74
Rutherford, Richard, 36-37
Ryder, Mark, 32

S
Sanasardo, Paul, 74, 83
Sarach, Marian, 72, 74, 75
School of Contemporary Dancers (Winnipeg), The, 49, 71-73, 82, 96, 103, 111, 113, 114, 133
  autonomy from Contemporary Dancers, 114
Shalom, 100, 119, 151
Sharonblue, 119, 154
Sherman, Suzette, 82
Shewchuk, Alana, 57, 111, 115, 116, 119, 122, 126, 137, 142
Shojani, Moti, 95, 96
Shout, 153
Six Messages, 129, 130, 154
Smith, Cherie, 61
Sokoloff, Ben. *See* Browne, Rachel, Sokoloff, Ben
Solitude, 84, 87, 106, 150
Solo for Christopher Gower, 152
Solov, Zachary, 32
Souster, Raymond, 61
Southam, Ann, 120, 125, 129, 135, 138, 144, 145
Spivak, Gloria, 24
Spohr, Arnold, 39, 40, 41, 43, 44, 62
Stagant, Ernie, 44
Stroud, Tom, 113-15
  double residencies, 114
Sunset Sentences, 106, 108, 109, 152
Surfield, Tom, 90

T
Take Five, 147
Taylor, Paul, 27, 144
Taylor-Corbett, Lynne, 83, 84, 89, 94
Tetley, Glen, 32
Theme and Rock, 149
Thomson, Faye, 49, 55, 72, 113, 114, 115, 132, 133
Thorvaldson, Olivia, 115
Three Faces of Jazz, 148
Three Square Pegs, 118
To the New Year, 103, 151
To the Year 2000, 104, 144, 150
Toward Light, 109, 117, 119, 124-27, 128, 129, 130, 133, 135, 136, 137, 154
Tres Bailes Enigmaticos, 106, 152
Tucker, David, 80
Tudor, Antony, 21-23
  psychological ballets and, 22
Turmoil, 53, 147

U
Unsworth, Karen, 93
Untitled, 150
Urge, The, 148

V
Variations, 71, 139, 149
Verdy, Violette, 26
Vesak, Norbert, 75, 83

W
Wagoner, Dan, 139
Walker, Norman, 70
Walling, Savannah, 102
Waring, James, 69-70, 72, 74
Wernick, Richard, 37
Where the Shining Trumpets Blow, 148
Williams, David, 78, 81
Williams, Don, 63
Willow Island retreat (Winnipeg), 15, 133
Willow Island, 132, 133, 155
Winter, Ethel, 32
Wolofsky, Zella, 80
Woman I Am, The, 80, 85, 87, 149
Woolen, Elizabeth, 42
Wyatt, Olivia, 40

Y
Young, Marilyn, 40, 43

Z
Ziebel, Shelley, 80, 89
Zuckerman, George, 68